Differentiating for Inclusion

Target Ladders:
Behavioural, Emotional and Social Difficulties

Rachel Foulger
Sue Smallwood
Marion Aust

Series editor Kate Ruttle

LDA has a range of learning development aids to help children with special needs and general learning difficulties. For our full range and helpful information, visit www.ldalearning.com.

Permission to photocopy

This book contains materials which may be reproduced by photocopier or other means for use by the purchaser. The permission is granted on the understanding that these copies will be used within the educational establishment of the purchaser. The book and all its contents remain copyright. Copies may be made without reference to the publisher or the licensing scheme for the making of photocopies operated by the Publishers' Licensing Agency.

The rights of Rachel Foulger, Sue Smallwood and Marion Aust to be identified as the authors of this work have been asserted in accordance with sections 77 and 78 of the Copyright, Designs and Patents Act of 1988.

Target Ladders: Behavioural, Emotional and Social Difficulties

ISBN 978-1-85503-551-5

© 2013 Rachel Foulger, Sue Smallwood and Marion Aust

All Rights Reserved

First published 2013

Reprinted 2014

Printed in the UK for LDA

LDA, Findel Education, Hyde Buildings, Ashton Road, Hyde, Cheshire, SK14 4SH

Contents

Introduction: Closing the gap — 4

Using Target Ladders
How to use this book — 6
Scope and Sequence charts — 11
Records of Progress — 18

BESD
What are BESD? — 22
Why do children have BESD? — 24
Building self-esteem — 27
Meeting the needs of BESD children in school — 29
The BESD-friendly classroom — 37
FAQs — 40

The Target Ladders
Aspect 1: Coping in the classroom — 48
Aspect 2: Unstructured times — 56
Aspect 3: Controlling emotions — 64
Aspect 4: Taking responsibility — 72
Aspect 5: Social interactions with peers — 80
Aspect 6: Managing transitions — 88

Links to other *Target Ladders* titles — 96
Other useful resources from LDA — 96

Closing the gap

Although schools are trying to reduce the number of children on their Special Educational Need (SEN) registers, the array of learning difficulties faced by the children is not changing or diminishing. In many areas, the responsibility for identifying learning difficulties and supporting the children is being thrust more onto schools because the external services hitherto available to support identification and remediation are fast disappearing. In most primary schools, the responsibility for tackling children's learning challenges continues to lie with class teachers and Special Educational Needs Coordinators (SENCos), many of whom are non-specialists.

Since 2012, reporting on children's behaviour and the way in which it is managed in schools has been a separate category in the Ofsted Evaluation Schedule. Behaviour, including attitude to learning, is now recognised as playing a significant part in children's learning. Inspectors are now looking for evidence that schools are working to 'close the gap' and that there is improvement in behaviour over time for children with particular behavioural needs. The first step in closing the gap is seeing beyond the problem behaviour, to focus on what the child is actually telling us by the behaviour.

Case study

A Year 4 child consistently refused to complete tasks and kept telling adults to *'go away and leave me alone'* when they tried to offer support. An analysis of when these behaviours occurred showed that this child was trying to work out what he had to do and was frustrated when adults kept interrupting his thought processes. What he needed was longer take-up time.

The child was given an 'I need help' card and shown how and when to use it. This allowed the child some independence in working and enabled the adults working with him to understand his needs. The strategy was used to help the child to reach his target of asking for help appropriately in lessons.

Whether individual targets are recorded on an Individual Education Plan (IEP), an internal target sheet, a Record of Progress or by some other mechanism, the fact remains that these children continue to need small-steps targets in order to clarify learning priorities and experience a sense of achievement when they tick off another target.

The *Target Ladders* books focus on one SEN at a time, in order that the range of difficulties and challenges facing young people with that SEN can be acknowledged. If any child in your care has any of the behaviours or difficulties addressed by a book in the series, then the targets listed in that book should be helpful and appropriate.

The *Target Ladders* books aim to support you in the following ways:

- Focusing on what a child can do, rather than what they cannot do, in order to identify next steps.
- Presenting 'small-steps' targets for children.
- Suggesting strategies and activities you may find helpful in order to achieve the targets.
- Giving you the information you need to use your professional judgement and understanding of the child in determining priorities for learning.
- Recognising that every child is different and will follow their own pathway through the targets.
- Giving you an overview of the range of difficulties experienced by children with a particular SEN. Not all children will experience all of the difficulties, but once you know and understand the implications of the SEN, it gives you a better understanding as to a child's learning priorities.
- Providing a system for setting and monitoring targets which can replace or complement IEPs.

Setting useful targets for a child can be tricky. But *'He's always misbehaving'* is not a constructive statement when deciding what the next steps should be. In order to support the child, you need to find out first what they can do already and then break down the next steps. You are then in a good position to set targets and consider interventions.

Case study

A very active Year 6 boy always liked to be first in line, often pushing and knocking others out of the way to get there. A simplistic target would have been to *'line up properly'* but this would have been too big a target and would have proved unachievable.

Breaking the target down meant that his first target was to *'line up in the position told'*, since picking numbers helped solve classroom arguments as to the position in which each child lined up. While he was working towards this target, work was done to improve his understanding of personal space. That enabled the next target to be *'don't get too close to others and keep your place in a moving line'*.

Using the *Target Ladders* books will enable both non-specialist teachers and SENCos to identify appropriate learning goals for independent learning, to adapt the suggested strategies or ideas for their own children and to begin to impact on the children's Behavioural, Emotional and Social Difficulties in order to close the gap between these children and their peers.

How to use this book

You will find a simple five-step summary of how to use this book on page 9.

Every child with Behavioural, Emotional and Social Difficulties (BESD) has different strengths and weaknesses. The priority for addressing these will be determined by the difficulties currently being faced by the child and will depend on your professional judgement, supported by the child's current anxieties.

To support you with focused target setting, the book is structured as follows:

- Six different Aspects of BESD have been identified (see Fig. 1 opposite). Think about the child's difficulties; which of these Aspects is causing most concern at the moment?
- Within each Aspect there are four different Target Ladders, each based on a particular area of challenge. This is intended to help you to think carefully about precisely where the barrier may be.
- The relevant Target Ladder can then be used to identify the 'next step' target for the child.
- Suggested activities and strategies offer classroom-friendly ideas so you can support the child to meet their target.

For example, as you can see in the chart opposite, difficulties with Aspect 2: Unstructured times can be subdivided into specific areas to work on: Understanding social expectations, Appropriate interactions, Managing conflict and Managing the play-to-work transition. Each Target Ladder contains 28 targets.

Aspects, Target Ladders and Targets

Aspects

The six different Aspects of BESD identified in this book describe contexts and difficulties which are frequently faced by children who struggle to manage aspects of their behaviours. In order to identify the most appropriate Aspect for a particular child, you will need to identify both the contexts which the child finds particularly challenging, and possible reasons for the difficult behaviour. If every behaviour is a communication, what is the child trying to communicate? The priority when deciding which of the Aspects is most important will come from an understanding of the child's current behaviours and where the most urgent challenges are presented.

The Aspects of BESD identified in this book are:

1. Coping in the classroom
2. Unstructured times
3. Controlling emotions
4. Taking responsibility
5. Social interactions with peers
6. Managing transitions.

Target Ladders

Each of the Aspects is further subdivided into four Target Ladders, each of which addresses different parts of the Aspect. These enable you to develop your understanding of the child's individual needs, 'drilling down' to assist you to identify the child's particular strengths and weaknesses. The Target Ladders are set out on pages 48–95.

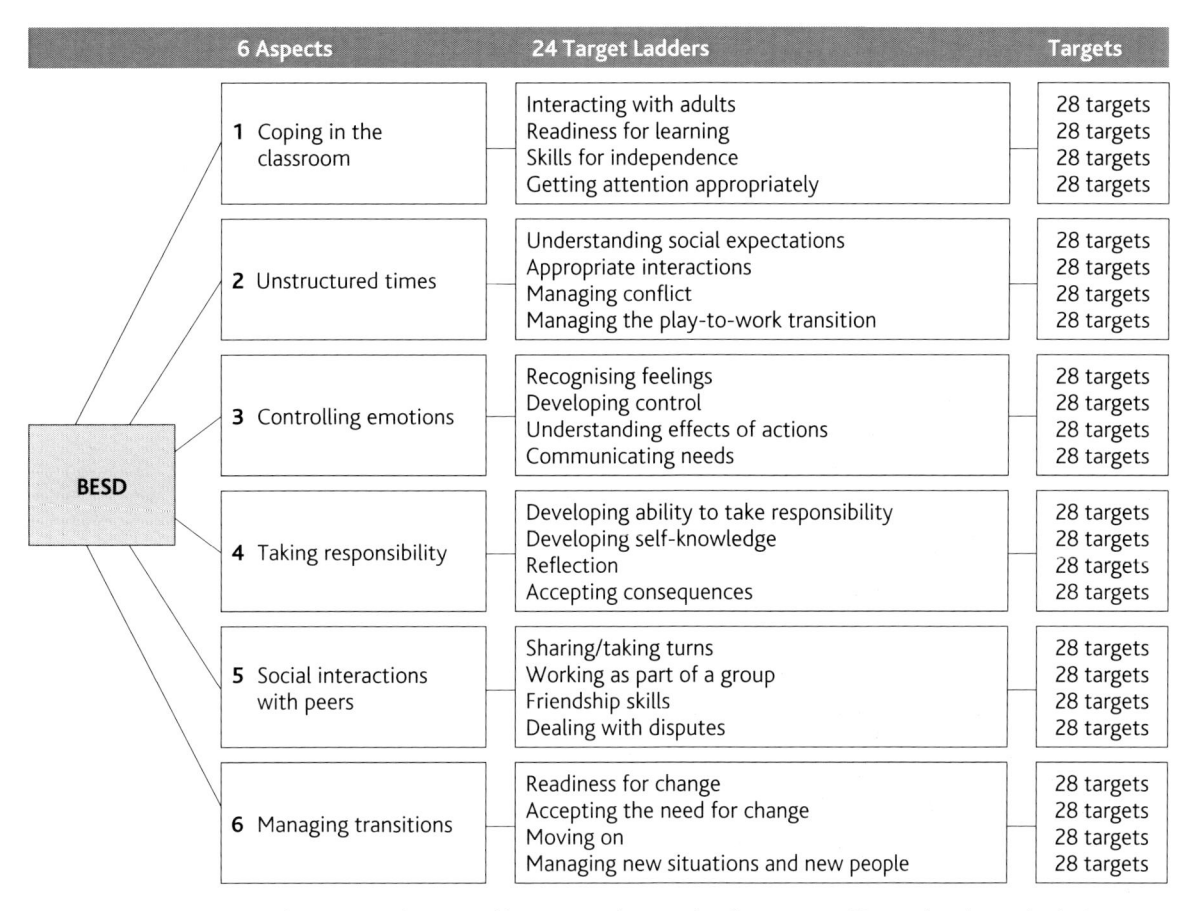

6 Aspects	24 Target Ladders	Targets
1 Coping in the classroom	Interacting with adults Readiness for learning Skills for independence Getting attention appropriately	28 targets 28 targets 28 targets 28 targets
2 Unstructured times	Understanding social expectations Appropriate interactions Managing conflict Managing the play-to-work transition	28 targets 28 targets 28 targets 28 targets
3 Controlling emotions	Recognising feelings Developing control Understanding effects of actions Communicating needs	28 targets 28 targets 28 targets 28 targets
4 Taking responsibility	Developing ability to take responsibility Developing self-knowledge Reflection Accepting consequences	28 targets 28 targets 28 targets 28 targets
5 Social interactions with peers	Sharing/taking turns Working as part of a group Friendship skills Dealing with disputes	28 targets 28 targets 28 targets 28 targets
6 Managing transitions	Readiness for change Accepting the need for change Moving on Managing new situations and new people	28 targets 28 targets 28 targets 28 targets

Fig. 1: The structure of *Target Ladders: BESD*. Each Aspect has four Target Ladders, each with 28 individual targets.

Targets

There are 28 targets in each Target Ladder, with the simplest labelled with the letter 'A', then moving through the alphabet up to 'N', which are the most difficult. In each Target Ladder, pairs of targets, identified by the same letter, present a similar level of challenge. So, for example, all of the targets marked E are at approximately the same level of development, which is slightly easier than F and slightly harder than D. Since each child is individual, some children will achieve harder targets before they do easier ones – and no child would be expected to work their way through all of the targets.

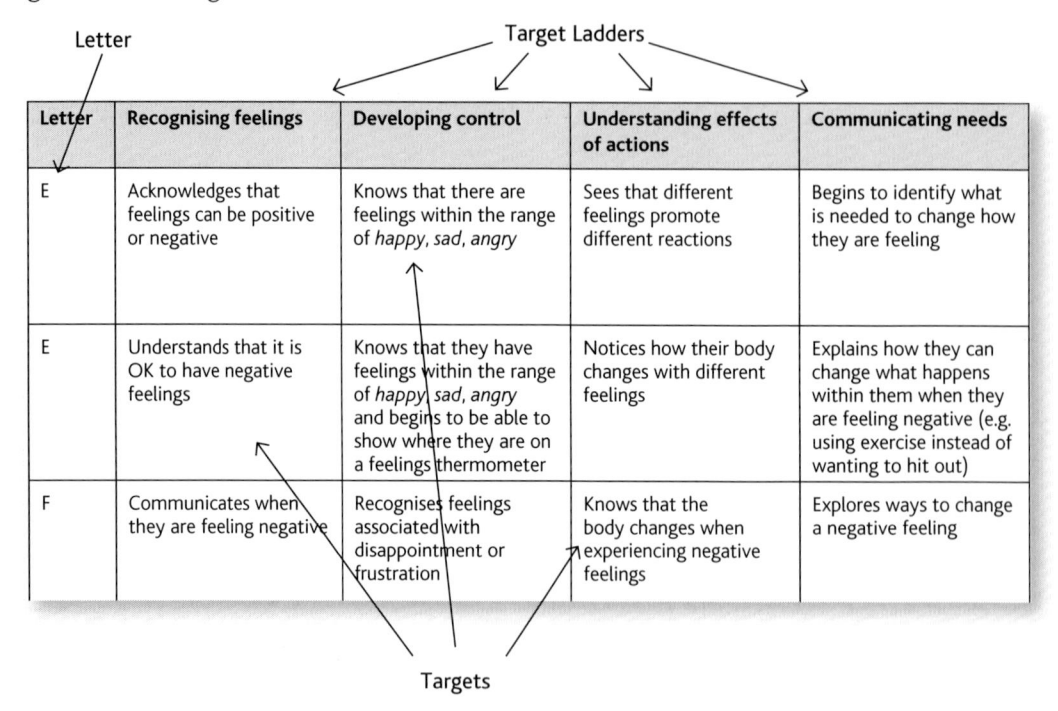

Letter	Recognising feelings	Developing control	Understanding effects of actions	Communicating needs
E	Acknowledges that feelings can be positive or negative	Knows that there are feelings within the range of *happy, sad, angry*	Sees that different feelings promote different reactions	Begins to identify what is needed to change how they are feeling
E	Understands that it is OK to have negative feelings	Knows that they have feelings within the range of *happy, sad, angry* and begins to be able to show where they are on a feelings thermometer	Notices how their body changes with different feelings	Explains how they can change what happens within them when they are feeling negative (e.g. using exercise instead of wanting to hit out)
F	Communicates when they are feeling negative	Recognises feelings associated with disappointment or frustration	Knows that the body changes when experiencing negative feelings	Explores ways to change a negative feeling

Fig. 2: Part of the Target Ladders table for Aspect 3: Controlling emotions (page 66), showing how targets are structured in the ladders.

However, it is not necessarily the case that the targets in row E for every Aspect are at the same developmental level, because the Aspects are so different. Thus, a child may have a target from row E in Aspect 3: Controlling emotions but a target from row H in Aspect 4: Taking responsibility.

The targets are all written in positive language. This is to support you when you:

- look through them to find out what the child *can already* do;
- use them as the basis of the target you set for the child.

As you track the statements through each ladder, identifying what the child can already do, be aware of missed steps. If a child has missed one of the steps, further progress up that ladder may be insecure. Many children learn to mask the missed step, using developing skills in other aspects to help them, but the time may come when the missed step will cause difficulties.

Activities and strategies to achieve the targets

In the Target Ladders on pages 48–95, targets are listed on left-hand pages. The corresponding right-hand pages offer ideas for activities and strategies that you might use to help to achieve the targets. These are suggestions only – but they have all been used successfully in classrooms and are accepted good practice. Here, however, the activities are shown at the point in the developmental process at which they are likely to make the most impact.

The suggested activities can often be adapted to work for a range of targets within this stage of the ladder. For this reason, activities are generally not linked to individual targets.

How to set targets: A five-step summary

1. **Use Fig. 1 on page 7 to identify the one or two Aspects of BESD which are most challenging for the child.**

2. **Turn to the Scope and Sequence charts on pages 11–17.** These charts will help you pinpoint the specific targets you need – a more detailed explanation is given on page 11. The Scope and Sequence charts show the *upper limit* of the targets reached in each Target Ladder in each Aspect. Use these to gain an indication of where in the book you are likely to find appropriate targets.

3. **In the Target Ladders tables on pages 48–95, locate the targets** that you have identified from the Scope and Sequence chart and pinpoint specific ones for the child to work towards.

4. **Photocopy or print out from the CD the relevant targets page** so that you can:
   - highlight and date those the child can already do;
   - identify the next priorities.

5. **Use the Record of Progress sheet on page 19 or on the CD** to create a copy of the targets for the child or their parents.

Making the most of Target Ladders

You may find the following tips helpful when setting your targets.

- If you are not sure which Aspect to highlight for a child:
  - think about your main concerns about that child's learning;
  - talk to the child about what they would like to improve;
  - discuss targets with the child's parents/carers.

  A target that the child wants to improve is more likely to be successful.

- Once you have identified the Aspect, use the Scope and Sequence charts on pages 11–17 to identify the most beneficial Target Ladder and ascertain on which page to start.
  - Look for any 'missed steps' and target those first. The child is likely to find success fairly quickly and will be motivated to continue to try to reach new targets.
  - Talk to the child and agree an appropriate target based on your skills inventory. Again, targets which the child is aware of tend to be achieved most quickly and are motivational.

- The target does not have to be the lowest unachieved statement in any ladder: use your professional judgement and knowledge of the child to identify the most useful and important target for the child.

- No child will follow all of the targets in precisely the order listed. Use your professional judgement and your knowledge about what the child can already do to identify the most appropriate target and be realistic in your expectations. There may be some zigzagging up and down a column.
- When setting targets, always ask yourself practical questions:
    - What can I change in order to enable the child to meet the targets?
    - What people and resources are available to support the child?
    - What is the likelihood of a child achieving a target within the next month or so?
    - What targets have been agreed with other children in the class?

It is important that the targets you set are realistic considering the time, the adult support and the resources available.

Once you have identified what the child can already achieve, continue to highlight and update the sheets each time the child achieves a new target. Celebrate progress with the child – while, at the same time, constantly checking to ensure that previously achieved targets remain secure. If any target becomes insecure, revisit it briefly without setting a formal target in order to give the child an opportunity to consolidate the skill without feeling that they are going backwards in their achievements.

Scope and Sequence charts

The Scope and Sequence charts can be used to help you to pinpoint targets, following the advice on the preceding pages. Once you have identified the Aspect(s) you wish to focus on:

1. Find the relevant page in the Scope and Sequence charts on pages 12–17. Look for the Aspect name here:

2. Identify the Target Ladder(s) that matches the skills you wish to target. Look for the names of the ladders here:

3. Read down the list of targets here: The target shown here will be one of the highest for the ladder on that page. If the target listed for the first page is too easy, look at the next target beneath it. Continue until you reach a target that is beyond the child's current attainment.

4. Find the page number, shown here: Turn to that page and read all the targets on it. One of them should be appropriate. If not, turn to the previous or subsequent page.

Scope and Sequence Aspect 5: Social interactions with peers

Friendship skills

Page	Letters	Target Ladder focus	Focus of suggestions
80	A–D	Asks if they can join in a small group having fun in the playground	Asking to join a group
82	E–H	Says one thing that they think makes someone 'a good friend'	A 'friendship book'
84	I–L	On occasions, will ask to join in games with children outside their immediate friendship circle	Exploring friendships
86	M–N	Accepts that different friends may have different qualities	Different people, different strengths

Dealing with disputes

Page	Letters	Target Ladder focus	Focus of suggestions
80	A–D	Says what they like and dislike doing	Using role-play to explore emotions
82	E–H	Feels able to say 'no' to another child	Saying 'no'
84	I–L	Shows resilience when other children are upset with them, by trying to identify what has gone wrong	Developing resilience
86	M–N	Is appropriately assertive in their dealings with others	Passive, aggressive, assertive

Fig. 3: Part of the Scope and Sequence chart for Aspect 5 (see page 16).

Bear in mind the following:

- The wording of the target may not be precisely accurate for your child. Modify it to make it appropriate.
- Different children may meet the target statements in a slightly different order. The order shown is approximate and true for many children. Adapt the order in which you set the targets for the individual child.
- No child is expected to have all of the targets on the page. A range of small-steps targets is shown in order to give you the widest possible variety of targets from which to select.
- If you cannot find a target which meets your needs, use the other targets to give you an idea of the level expected and write your own target. It is important that all of the targets on the Record of Progress are appropriate for the individual child.

Scope and Sequence Aspect 1: Coping in the classroom

Interacting with adults

Page	Letters	Target Ladder focus	Focus of suggestions
48	A–D	Tells an adult as soon as something happens	Forming relationships
50	E–H	Knows that talking with adults can have positive outcomes (praise) or negative outcomes (consequences)	Praise and consequences
52	I–L	Asks an adult to act as mediator to sort out difficulties with other children	Building relationships
54	M–N	Talks to adults appropriately in a range of situations	Sharing worries about moving to a new class or school

Readiness for learning

Page	Letters	Target Ladder focus	Focus of suggestions
48	A–D	Talks about what they are doing	Classroom routines
50	E–H	Finds solutions to problems using ideas from teacher input	Problem-solving
52	I–L	Sees setbacks as a way of moving on	Bouncing back
54	M–N	Is keen to take on the challenge of moving to secondary school	Pupil passports

Skills for independence

Page	Letters	Target Ladder focus	Focus of suggestions
48	A–D	Moves around the classroom to different directed activities	Classroom routines
50	E–H	Sorts out own resources to solve a particular problem	Building co-operation skills
52	I–L	Has the resilience to know how to cope with a setback	Bouncing back
54	M–N	Organises self to be ready for secondary school	Reflecting

Getting attention appropriately

Page	Letters	Target Ladder focus	Focus of suggestions
48	A–D	Knows the names of all children and adults and uses them correctly	Learning names
50	E–H	Knows that negative attention-seeking behaviours have a consequence	Praise and consequences
52	I–L	Talks about what they could do next time and is able to act on it	Following the rules
54	M–N	Talks about what has helped/not helped at school	Reflecting

Scope and Sequence Aspect 2: Unstructured times

Understanding social expectations

Page	Letters	Target Ladder focus	Focus of suggestions
56	A–D	Follows the rules of a simple board game or playground game without adult support	Board games
58	E–H	Understands they have to co-operate with others when playing in the playground	Understanding conduct rules
60	I–L	Takes a leading role when playing a game in the playground with others	Playground friends
62	M–N	Volunteers for a position of social responsibility	Taking part in group work

Appropriate interactions

Page	Letters	Target Ladder focus	Focus of suggestions
56	A–D	Says 'Can I play with you please?' to another child	Joining in with games
58	E–H	Requests a turn with equipment politely	Social Stories™
60	I–L	Invites others to join them in playground activities	Playground friends / Positive 'post-playtimes'
62	M–N	Helps newcomers integrate socially	Making and breaking friends

Managing conflict

Page	Letters	Target Ladder focus	Focus of suggestions
56	A–D	Names feelings *friendly*, *proud* and demonstrates awareness of what they mean	Naming feelings
58	E–H	Is able to resist the temptation to join in with unwanted behaviour	Choices and consequences
60	I–L	Uses 'I' statements to express their views and opinions	'I' statements
62	M–N	Engages in restorative approaches	Principles of Restorative Justice

Managing the play-to-work transition

Page	Letters	Target Ladder focus	Focus of suggestions
56	A–D	Accepts the end of an activity when given a minute's warning	Now and Next boards
58	E–H	Accepts a consequence if they do not line up as directed	Choices and consequences
60	I–L	Shows enthusiasm for classroom-based activities	Becoming positive
62	M–N	Responds to verbal or non-verbal cues from the teacher that signal readiness for learning	Signals for learning

Scope and Sequence Aspect 3: Controlling emotions

Recognising feelings

Page	Letters	Target Ladder focus	Focus of suggestions
64	A–D	Can say when they were *happy, sad, angry* and explain what it felt like in their body	Talking about feelings
66	E–H	Names a full range of feelings and knows what it means to feel them	Where do you feel it?
68	I–L	Knows which actions will enhance or diminish feelings	Saying '*You've hurt my feelings*'
70	M–N	Can confidently say how they feel in a range of age-appropriate situations	Building social confidence

Developing control

Page	Letters	Target Ladder focus	Focus of suggestions
64	A–D	Links events to a particular feeling	Knowing what makes you feel better
66	E–H	Sorts feelings into categories	Sorting feelings
68	I–L	Knows what helps when they are feeling a particular emotion, and acts accordingly	Self-awareness
70	M–N	Can be in control through self-knowledge	Building social confidence

Understanding effects of actions

Page	Letters	Target Ladder focus	Focus of suggestions
64	A–D	Begins to grasp the idea that an action may change how they are feeling	Recognising feelings in pictures or photographs
66	E–H	Says when they might have a particular feeling	Using feelings thermometers
68	I–L	Knows how to manage their feelings in a positive and safe way	Dealing with conflict
70	M–N	Reacts appropriately to others	Learning respect

Communicating needs

Page	Letters	Target Ladder focus	Focus of suggestions
64	A–D	Can say what will make them feel calmer, before they get angry	Recognising body signals
66	E–H	Offers own ideas to change a negative feeling	Exercise and relaxation
68	I–L	Acts on the way that makes them feel differently (self-calms)	Positive thinking
70	M–N	Accepts who they are in relationships with others	Building relationships

Scope and Sequence Aspect 4: Taking responsibility

Developing ability to take responsibility

Page	Letters	Target Ladder focus	Focus of suggestions
72	A–D	Talks about or draws their version of events	Take the time
74	E–H	Works independently in age-related activities	Giving responsibilities
76	I–L	Takes responsibility for being a friend	Friendships
78	M–N	Confidently says what they are good at/less good at	Self-confidence

Developing self-knowledge

Page	Letters	Target Ladder focus	Focus of suggestions
72	A–D	Finds best way to say or draw what happened	Incident resolution
74	E–H	Understands that they are important and have self-worth	'Star of the week' Giving responsibilities
76	I–L	Knows what makes them and others a good friend	Friendships
78	M–N	Sees differences in self and others as positive attributes	Same and different

Reflection

Page	Letters	Target Ladder focus	Focus of suggestions
72	A–D	Explains to others what happened and begins to think about why	Take the time
74	E–H	Understands that choices can be good or bad	Being honest
76	I–L	Tolerates a range of people	Consequences
78	M–N	Is able to reflect on how differences affect social interactions	Social situations

Accepting consequences

Page	Letters	Target Ladder focus	Focus of suggestions
72	A–D	Realises that others may have their own version of events	Incident resolution
74	E–H	Understands that a different choice will make different things happen	Making choices
76	I–L	Gets involved in activities with others	Reflection
78	M–N	Accepts themselves for who they are	Self-confidence

Scope and Sequence Aspect 5: Social interactions with peers

Sharing/taking turns

Page	Letters	Target Ladder focus	Focus of suggestions
80	A–D	Takes turns, with one other person, according to the rules of a simple board game or playground game	Turn-taking games
82	E–H	Listens, in turn, to others making suggestions for games or classroom activities	Rules for listening
84	I–L	Offers support to others whose views they share in a decision-making process	Learning to listen without interrupting
86	M–N	Begins to make decisions, based on shared friendships and interests, how they could manage their free time in and out of school	Joining new groups

Working as part of a group

Page	Letters	Target Ladder focus	Focus of suggestions
80	A–D	Takes turns, in a group of three, at placing pieces of a medium-sized jigsaw	Jigsaw puzzles
82	E–H	With support, identifies ways in which the group can co-operate to achieve a task	Share stories
84	I–L	Suggests ways of achieving a group task	Group roles
86	M–N	Engages in a variety of group activities in and out of school	Joining new groups

Friendship skills

Page	Letters	Target Ladder focus	Focus of suggestions
80	A–D	Asks if they can join in a small group having fun in the playground	Asking to join a group
82	E–H	Says one thing that they think makes someone '*a good friend*'	A 'friendship book'
84	I–L	On occasions, will ask to join in games with children outside their immediate friendship circle	Exploring friendships
86	M–N	Accepts that different friends may have different qualities	Different people, different strengths

Dealing with disputes

Page	Letters	Target Ladder focus	Focus of suggestions
80	A–D	Says what they like and dislike doing	Using role-play to explore emotions
82	E–H	Feels able to say '*no*' to another child	Saying '*no*'
84	I–L	Shows resilience when other children are upset with them, by trying to identify what has gone wrong	Developing resilience
86	M–N	Is appropriately assertive in their dealings with others	Passive, aggressive, assertive

Scope and Sequence Aspect 6: Managing transitions

Readiness for change

Page	Letters	Target Ladder focus	Focus of suggestions
88	A–D	Identifies something they would like to do that they have not yet tried	Selecting activities
90	E–H	Says things they think they can do well	Pupil passports
92	I–K	Is willing to 'have a go' at something they are unsure of achieving	Community challenge
94	L–N	Carries out duties of assigned roles with competence and confidence	A solution-focused approach

Accepting the need for change

Page	Letters	Target Ladder focus	Focus of suggestions
88	A–D	Follows routines for movement around the classroom	Establish routines
90	E–H	Says what things they will do better with the change of year group	Pupil passports
92	I–K	Talks to adults about their worries and hopes for the change of year group	Managing anxiety
94	L–N	Anticipates the positive aspects of moving to secondary school	A solution-focused approach

Moving on

Page	Letters	Target Ladder focus	Focus of suggestions
88	A–D	Starts task when whole class directed by teacher	Staying on task
90	E–H	Accepts praise and works towards rewards	Descriptive praise
92	I–K	Shows determination to try something new	The language of goal-setting
94	L–N	Takes leading roles in some activities in and out of school	A solution-focused approach

Managing new situations and new people

Page	Letters	Target Ladder focus	Focus of suggestions
88	A–D	Uses a timer without support to sustain concentration for 4 minutes on a specific task	Using timers
90	E–H	Gets on well with most children in the class	Social scripts
92	I–K	Is helpful and considerate towards adults and children in the class	Community challenge
94	L–N	Is welcoming and accepting of new staff and class members	A solution-focused approach

Records of Progress

Creating a Record of Progress

Arrange to meet with the child and ask them first to tell you what they are good at. Record their responses on the Record of Progress (RoP). A blank form is supplied for you to copy on page 19 and on the CD. Ask them then to tell you which areas they would most like to improve. If it is appropriate, choose something that addresses at least one of their issues as a target so that the child feels some ownership of their RoP. If your school operates a pupil passport system then you may want to amend the RoP form, but you will nonetheless need a sheet that can be annotated and amended.

As you add one or two more targets, talk to the child to check that they agree that each target is relevant and that they understand what they will need to do to achieve their targets. Targets that children do not know or care about are much harder for them to achieve. Limit the number of targets to a maximum of three. Remember, you do not need to use the precise wording of the targets given here: adapt the words to match the maturity and understanding of the learner.

If you are planning to use a published BESD intervention, check to see what the recommended length of time for the intervention is. Monitor the impact of the intervention (see page 20) and review at regular intervals – at least half-termly – to see if there is an impact. If not, consider whether a different intervention would be more effective.

Principles for the effective use of an RoP include the following:

- The form must be 'live'. The child will need to have access to it at all times, as will all adults who work with the child, in order that it can be referred to, amended and updated regularly. It would be good practice to send a copy home for the parents/carers. If you think that the child is likely to lose or destroy their RoP, make a photocopy so that you can supply another.
- Together with the child, you have identified their priority areas to focus on. Management and support for these should be consistent across the school day and from all adults.
- As soon as each target has been achieved, according to the success criteria you agreed, the form should be dated and a 'next step' considered.
- When you set up the RoP, select a review date which is ideally about half a term ahead and no more than one term ahead. Do not wait until this date to identify that targets have been achieved, but on this date review progress towards all targets – or identified next steps – and agree new targets.
- If a target has not been achieved, consider why not. If possible, try a different approach to meeting the target. Having the same target over and over is likely to bore the child and put them off following their RoP.

RECORD OF PROGRESS

Name _____ Class _____ Date agreed _____ Review date _____

My targets are	I will know that I have achieved my target when I can	Date when I achieved my target	Next steps
I am good at			
I would like to be better at			
It helps me when			

RoP number: _____ Targets approved by: Pupil _____ Teacher _____

SENCo _____ Parent/Carer _____ TA _____

Monitoring a Record of Progress

In order to ensure that your Record of Progress (RoP) is used effectively, you need to monitor progress towards the targets each time you offer support. Use a monitoring sheet; a photocopiable example is given on page 21 and on the CD.

- Use a separate sheet – copied on to a different colour of paper – for each target.
- Write the child's name at the top of the sheet and the target underneath.
- On each occasion when someone works with the child towards the target, they should write the smaller, more specific target that you are working towards *during this session* in the box.
- They should then write a comment. On each occasion the child achieves the target during the session and then back in class, tick the box.

Comments should, as far as possible, refer to the child's behaviour and attitude rather than to their learning, which should be celebrated during the session. The intention is that these sheets should be used to create a cumulative record of a child's progress towards their target. The evidence here can be used to assess the impact of an intervention in order that its appropriateness can be evaluated swiftly and any additional actions can be taken promptly.

What precisely you record will depend on the type of support being offered and the nature of the target.

- If you are delivering a planned intervention, make a record of the unit/page/activity and a comment about the learning the child demonstrated. For example, a comment relating to a target about the child's ability to manage their temper might be: '*Understands use of feelings strip*'.
- If you are offering support in the classroom, you might want to comment on the child's learning over a few lessons. Focus on what the child has achieved in the lessons and whether the learning is secure.
- As a general principle, aim to include more positive than negative comments, and always try to balance a negative with a positive comment.

At the half-termly review of the RoP, collect together all of the monitoring sheets and look at the frequency of the comments against each target as well as the learning they reflect. If a child has had absences, or an intervention has not happened as often as planned, consider what impact that has had on the effectiveness of the intervention. If the intervention has gone as planned, look at the progress charted and ask yourself these questions:

- Is it swift enough? Is the intervention helping this child to close the gap? Is the adult working with the child the best person for the job?
- Is this the best intervention? Is there anything else you can reasonably do in school?
- What should happen next? If the intervention was successful, do you continue it, develop it, consolidate it or change to a different target?

At the end of the process, create a new RoP with the child and make a new monitoring sheet.

Monitoring the progress of _____ towards meeting

Target _____

Date	Target	Comment	Achieved			

What are BESD?

The British Psychological Society (BPS) states that:

> Whether a child or young person is considered to have BESD depends on a range of factors, including the nature, frequency, persistence, severity and abnormality of the difficulties and their cumulative effect on the child or young person's behaviour and/or emotional wellbeing compared with what might generally be expected for a particular age.

(*The Education of Children and Young People with Behavioural, Emotional and Social Difficulties as a Special Educational Need*, DCSF, 2008)

Behavioural, Emotional and Social Difficulties (BESD) is an umbrella term covering a range of difficulties that can affect a child's ability to access the school curriculum. Behavioural issues can be a symptom of, or can mask, another underlying difficulty.

Children with BESD respond to school in a variety of ways. Some are volatile and unpredictable with no discernible triggers. Other children may appear to be passive and accepting, but then have an unexpected and disproportionate response to a challenge. This can be compared to 'milk boiling over' – the warning signs are often subtle, and appear trivial, so that the eventual outburst appears to come from nowhere – and is very hard to manage in the classroom, as the child does not always recognise their own growing level of frustration or how to manage their responses in a non-damaging way.

A significant factor for all children with BESD is that they may also have some form of learning difficulty. The learning difficulty may be a cause of attention-seeking behaviour as children soon learn to distract attention from the learning, which they cannot manage, to the behaviour. Setting achievable work and putting in place interventions which support the learning increase the chances of making a positive impact on the child's behaviour. It is much more common to find that learning difficulty is the root cause of poor behaviour rather than the behaviour impeding the progress of the learning.

BESD indicators

The following list is not intended to be used as an assessment tool. Instead, it groups behaviours into different areas of likely difficulty. Understanding these groupings may help you to approach them more appropriately. Targets in this book are appropriate for use with children who display challenging behaviours, whatever the reason: an explanation for a behaviour should not be accepted as an excuse.

Behavioural
Refuses to accept, and comply with, rules, routines and adult direction, both in and out of the classroom.
Is unable to manage own responses and take responsibility for own actions.
Lacks self-awareness and self-control.
Displays rudeness.
Verbally or physically abuses adults and peers. In the classroom, this may be seen as insolence, verbal abuse, aggressive responses, inappropriate language (swearing) and/or physical and threatening behaviour.

Emotional
May be angry, withdrawn, sad, mistrustful or clingy.
Is demanding of adult time.
Is resistant to support, advice and guidance from adults.
Is unable to recognise feelings in self and others and respond appropriately (lacks empathy).
Often responds to events disproportionately.
Exhibits anger, which may be due to developmental delay (responses may have been learnt at an earlier stage of development, for example as a toddler, and are now habituated).
May show an attachment disorder, temper, frustration or an underlying (and sometimes unidentified) learning difficulty. The child may have emotionally unresponsive parents and misreads emotions, not having learned acceptable responses at an early age.

Social
Lacks social understanding.
Has difficulty in sharing (toys, games, adult time).
Is unable to successfully manage relationships with other children.
Responds inappropriately to other children.
Is demanding of adult time.
Is unable to recognise social cues or distinguish between adults and children, treating them all the same.

Why do children have BESD?

There are a myriad of reasons for children to show BESD. The most common are linked to early experiences outside of school or to learning difficulties at school, but there are also other conditions which are linked to BESD (see Table 1 on pages 25–26). It should also be acknowledged that some children develop challenging behaviours as a response to frustration from the start of formal education, when they have not been ready or able to understand either the demands of the classroom or what they are expected to learn.

Before they start school, or during their time at school, many children will have difficult experiences at home. These include the arrival of a baby, bereavement, divorce, caring for a family member, domestic violence, frequent house moves, high parental expectations, lack of parental interest, and so on. Vulnerable children in particular may deal with difficult experiences out of school by adopting unacceptable or withdrawn behaviours in school. Children need to be taught acceptable ways to seek support in managing their feelings and behaviour, using agreed and acceptable responses.

Starting school

When a child starts their formal education, they bring their own complex personal history; but it is useful to consider the range of skills, attitudes and experiences that will enable any child to be successful during their school years.

Children who are successful in school

A successful child will feel *confident* that school is the right place to be and that the key adults in their life are united in their *approval* of them as learners and members of the school community. They will have the necessary *resilience* to manage the changes and challenges ahead of them. They will be *sociable*, able to *play* and be *happy* when winning or losing games. They will show curiosity about the world and *trust* the adults in school to make decisions about their learning.

For the successful child, school is seen as an exciting, interesting, stimulating and agreeable place to be; the child will be happy to share their daily experiences with both parents and school staff, who will listen in a non-judgemental and approving manner.

Children with BESD

Children with BESD do not always see school as a happy place to be. They may lack confidence in themselves as learners and develop strategies to avoid work they may not understand. They may:

- have difficulty with the social aspects of school life, finding the imposition of rules and routines unwanted;
- have no previous experience of firm boundaries, or of having to share adult time with a group of peers;
- lack the resilience to manage the hustle and bustle of a busy classroom;
- have a medical condition that affects their ability to manage the classroom.

Some children may have had to be independent from an early age and may have developed an inflated sense of self, feeling that they have to solve any problems themselves. Children with some forms of BESD often have a heightened sense of fairness and may subsequently become the class bully because they feel that wrongdoers have not been adequately or equally punished.

Diagnoses

There are a range of diagnoses, often associated with BESD, which need to be made by a pediatrician or psychologist. Some of the most common diagnoses found in schools today are shown in Table 1 below, with some sources for further information. (The websites listed here are suggestions only – there are many others.)

Diagnosis	Background	Characteristic behaviours
Attachment disorder	There are ten key emotional needs that are necessary for all humans to manage their emotions effectively: attention, acceptance, appreciation, encouragement, affection, respect, support, comfort, approval and security. A secure attachment is formed when an infant has these needs met and reciprocates them with a care-giver. Insecure attachments can form when one or more of these needs are not met. More information can be found at sites such as www.attachmentdisorder.net	• May be over-clingy or very independent • Is overly affectionate or shows a dislike of affection • Seeks attention or is withdrawn • Constantly seeks reassurance or is unable to cope with getting anything wrong
Attention Deficit Hyperactivity Disorder (ADHD) or Attention Deficit Disorder (ADD)	These are biological or medical conditions, which affect the chemicals that transmit impulses to the frontal lobe of the brain. Children with ADD have a similar set of behaviours to those with ADHD, but with a lack of noticeable hyperactivity. More information can be found at www.adhd.org.uk	• Has poor social skills • Has low self-esteem • Achievement is inconsistent • Does not pay attention to details • Is easily distracted • Has a poor memory • Has auditory perception difficulties • Struggles to plan ahead • Is easily bored • Has poor self-organisational skills • Is always 'on the go'
Oppositional Defiance Disorder (ODD)	ODD is the term used to describe disruptive and oppositional behaviour that is particularly directed towards authority figures, such as parents or teachers. More information can be found at www.netdoctor.co.uk/adhd/oppositionaldefiantdisorders.htm	• Is quick-tempered • Is argumentative • Is defiant • Annoys others • Blames others for their mistakes • Is often angry, resentful, spiteful or vindictive

Diagnosis	Background	Characteristic behaviours
Autistic Spectrum (AS) and Asperger Syndrome	This term describes a range of difficulties that children experience, because they have a different view of the world. A diagnosis of AS would be based on identification of the 'Triad of impairment': • Social communication: difficulties in understanding verbal and non-verbal language; • Social interaction: difficulties in recognising their own and others' feelings (empathy); • Social imagination: difficulties in understanding and predicting other people's behaviour and intentions and imagining situations outside their world. Asperger Syndrome is classed as a form of autism. AS children may be very able but have difficulties in school consistent with their different understanding of the world around them. More information can be found at www.autism.org.uk	• Is self-directed • Is obsessive • Is uninterested in others' emotional responses • Has difficulty in processing information • Is aggressive (pinches, hits, slaps) • Spits or bites • Runs away • Has temper tantrums • Displays anxiety • Wants to participate only according to their own rules • Has poor understanding of social rules • Does not read body language, facial expression, tone of voice • Does not understand idioms • Appears rude/insensitive
Foetal Alcohol Syndrome (FAS)	Some children are affected by pre-birth development, particularly in relation to drug and alcohol misuse during pregnancy. This can lead to difficulties in the development of the brain and can impact on later physical and emotional development. More information can be found at the Foetal Alcohol Syndrome website www.fasaware.co.uk	• Does not fit in well or mix well • Does not follow rules • Is easily led • Does not learn from mistakes • Always wants to be the centre of attention • Talks too much • Is impulsive • Shows frustration • Has difficulty separating fantasy and reality

Table 1: Conditions that may be associated with BESD. Such diagnoses need to be made by a pediatrician or an educational psychologist.

There are many other reasons for children's poor behaviour in school, including a range of other diagnoses, children's experience of abusive behaviour and a feeling of anger at the world.

A diagnosis should be seen as a reason, not an excuse, for bad or inappropriate behaviour. However, understanding any underlying condition will help a teacher to make appropriate 'reasonable adjustments' to accommodate the child's special educational needs.

Building self-esteem

The term 'self-esteem' is used to describe the way a child feels about themselves and incorporates feelings of self-confidence, resilience, self-value, self-respect and self-worth.

All of us, both adults and children alike, function more effectively if we are happy and feel good about ourselves. If a child has experienced high levels of negativity or failure before starting school and then experiences further failure in learning or social situations in school, then their sense of self will be low and this can impact on their attitude and behaviour both in and out of class as well as their relationships with others. They may also feel that there is little or no point in 'being good' as their experiences tell them they are never good enough; so they may increase the negative behaviours.

Some children with BESD will appear to have high self-esteem, but also have low feelings of self-worth, which are shown by their challenging behaviour in class. The development of self-esteem is a common thread running through all the Aspects in this book.

Self-esteem	A psychological term to describe a person's sense of self-worth or personal value. It involves an appraisal of their own appearance, beliefs, emotions and behaviour.
Self-worth	Having a favourable opinion of oneself; feeling worthy of respect.
Self-respect	A person's regard for the dignity of their own character and acceptance of who they are.
Self-value	A person's values overall, including beliefs and cultural values.
Self-confidence	A person's self-assurance in their judgement of their own capabilities.

Table 2: Some useful terms and synonyms for self-esteem.

How can we improve a child's self-esteem?

- Develop a positive classroom ethos, based on improving success through praise, honesty and challenge, so that every child knows that they are a valued member of the group.
- Build learning experiences which are based on a sound knowledge of each child's prior learning and which encourage independence.
- Provide activities that help children develop empathy; make sure that groups are changed for different activities so that children do not always work with the same children and are positively encouraged to work as a team, recognising that we all have different strengths.
- Build self-confidence; encourage children to have a 'can do' attitude and reinforce the understanding that we learn more effectively if we have

tried and failed, so every time we do something we gradually improve. Link learning in the classroom to early skills such as learning to walk. We all had to fall down a lot before we could master walking! Or look at the amount of time that athletes spend training, and the constant effort that is needed for them to perform at their best.

- Listen to the child and respond positively. Acknowledge any anxieties they may express and encourage a positive, 'can do' approach. If children wish to talk about difficulties at home, listen attentively (ensuring that you follow the school's Safeguarding procedures, and being alert to disclosures). Also, be confident that you can offer reassurance that the classroom is a safe place for each child to talk honestly about their concerns, where their concerns will be acknowledged, and solutions found where possible.

- Understand the need for children to develop resilience. Resilience is a term used to describe a set of qualities that foster a process of successful adaptation despite risk and adversity. We are all born with an innate capacity for resilience, by which we are able to develop social competence, problem-solving skills, a critical consciousness and a sense of purpose. For the troubled child, these skills may not all be in place or may be under-developed, so this will hinder their capacity to manage the social constraints and academic challenges of the classroom.

- Enable children to see that there are solutions to problems and that they can do better next time, even if they have been in trouble for their actions. A helpful tool to use following poor behaviour is an 'A, B, C' chart, which has three columns with the headings Antecedent, Behaviour and Consequence.
  - The **Antecedent** is the event that occurs immediately before the behaviour.
  - The **Behaviour** needs to be described in a specific way.
  - The **Consequence** is the outcome of the event.

  This is a useful de-briefing tool to help children understand the causes and consequences of the behaviour choices they have made; again, the focus should be on improvement. In other words: *'You have made the wrong choice this time, but you can do better next time'*.

- Understand the stress response. Many children with BESD are constantly in a high state of emotional arousal and are hyper-vigilant, so the adrenaline-fuelled stress response – the 'fight or flight' response – will kick in much earlier than for the more confident child. The stress response was first described almost 100 years ago as a theory that animals react to threats with a response from the sympathetic nervous system. It is a physical reaction to threat, either real or perceived. A release of adrenaline leads to one of four possible responses: fight, flight, freeze or flock. For the individual child, the response to pressure could be verbal or physical abuse (fight) or silence and withdrawal (flight). The adult must be aware that with either state, it is very difficult for a child to reason and explain why they did whatever they have done. So the question *'why?'* will not be easy for them to answer. It is better to allow time for the stress level to reduce, then use a method such as the 'A, B, C' chart described above, and enable the child to find ways to manage their behaviour better next time.

Meeting the needs of BESD children in school

Children have different levels of need and demands, which must be met in a fair and equitable way in school. It is important that each child feels safe and welcome in the classroom. Teaching and support staff time should be available to all children, not just the most demanding.

It is not helpful for any child to have undivided adult attention; all children should learn to be independent, and this will not develop if they expect the adults to be constantly on hand to guide them through all work at all times and to solve all problems for them.

In order to create a safe and secure classroom environment with effective classroom management you will need:

- rules, boundaries and high expectations (below);
- well-established routines (page 30);
- differentiated and appropriate learning and teaching (page 31);
- a focus on positive behaviours for learning (page 31);
- strategies for developing an emotionally literate class (page 32);
- a whole-school approach (page 34);
- strategies for effective ways of working with parents (page 35).

Rules, boundaries and high expectations

Establish the ground rules for the class at the start of the year and reinforce them at regular intervals. Bill Rogers (*Behaviour Management, A Whole School Approach*, Sage Publications, 2007) says that it is important that the children are involved in this exercise and have input into both rewards and sanctions.

Have consistently high expectations of positive behaviour and attitudes from everyone in the classroom, both children and adults. A mutually respectful relationship may need to be taught to some children, but should be reinforced to everyone on a daily basis. All adults working in the school should model positive and respectful relationships towards each other so that children can see good relationships in action constantly.

Ensure that all children are treated fairly and listened to; this may take some time to embed in a class at the start of the year, but once the children know that their teacher and support staff will listen to their concerns, then a trusting relationship can be developed.

Confidence, clarity and consistency (the 3Cs)

As the class teacher, you need to be *confident* in your approach to all children in your class, particularly those who challenge your authority. Children benefit from a *clear*, strong guide from the teacher, who can provide the security of firm and fair boundaries that are applied *consistently* in all circumstances. All adults should use the 3Cs to ensure that there is a safe and secure classroom ethos at all times.

Speech and body language

In social interaction, body language and tone of voice are at least as important as the words spoken: if the speaker looks and sounds aggressive, their words will be interpreted as aggressive by the listener. When we respond to a challenge to our authority, our non-verbal communication tends to appear aggressive and children respond to that more than to the words we say, however reasonable and supportive those words may be. In response, a child's behaviour can quickly escalate into temper tantrums or aggression, particularly if the child has low self-esteem or is a BESD child with a history of insecurity and a short fuse.

There are three different styles of communication: passive, aggressive and assertive.

- **Passive**. In this type of behaviour, people are always trying to please others and avoid conflict at all costs. They may have a meek, compliant and long-suffering attitude and use phrases such as, '*If you wouldn't mind*', '*Sorry to bother you*', and '*Is that all right?*'
  Adults in school using passive communication will not be able to use the 3Cs to communicate, thus leaving the child without a confident adult who can be trusted to make the right decisions about their learning.
- **Aggressive**. Aggressive people tend to bully other people and step on the rights of others in order to protect their own. They often come across as domineering or forceful. Phrases such as, '*You'd better ...*', '*You're a typical ...*' or '*Stupid ...*' are common parts of their speech. Body language can also indicate aggressive communicators: clenched fists, finger-pointing, leaning forward and glaring, and talking loudly are such signs.
  Adults using this style will often appear to have a well-behaved and orderly class, but they will not help the BESD child in the long run as they are ruling the class by fear, thus denying the chance for trusting and positive relationships to flourish and successful learning to take place.
- **Assertive**. Assertive communicators are clear, direct and honest. They are often described as thoughtful, optimistic, rational and decisive. They use phrases such as, '*I want ...*', '*I feel ...*', '*Let's do ...*' and '*What do you think?*' Their body language reflects their self-confidence – they stand straight and steady, and speak clearly with assurance.

All adults in school should aim to use an assertive communication style with both children and adults. Clear, open and honest communication helps to provide the safe and secure environment needed by all in school, most especially the troubled and troubling children.

Well-established routines

Routine, routine, routine. Routines and predictability are vital in the primary classroom. Many children have difficulties managing any changes in routines, even pleasant ones!

- Establish time and routines for the start and end of learning sessions. Pre-warn the class when a work session is about to end. For example, say, '*In five minutes I will ask you to finish*'; '*You have one minute left*'. Again, this has to be taught, and reinforced on a daily basis.

- There should be times when the demanding child learns coping strategies by working with other children, or by being given the time to work things out by themselves. For example, they can use techniques such as '1,2,3':
    1. try yourself;
    2. ask a friend;
    3. ask an adult.
- Build in time for toilet breaks.
- Allow a settling-in time after breaks and enable any break-time issues to be heard and dealt with as soon as possible after the event, or at a suitable time later in the day. Use active listening (see page 34) and Restorative Justice (see page 35) to solve any disputes swiftly and effectively.
- Also, establish routines for playtimes and unstructured times, giving special thought to agreed rules for playtime football.

Differentiated and appropriate learning and teaching

Children will enjoy school more and behave more appropriately if their work is interesting, clearly understood and of an achievable yet challenging level. Work should be planned based on a sound knowledge of each child so that they can develop confidence in themselves as both independent and collaborative learners. In general, planning to work from the known to the unknown is the most effective way forward. Target the use of 'catch up' programmes as well as the use of classroom support staff; it is preferable for all children to work with both the teacher and TAs during the course of the week.

A focus on positive behaviours for learning

The vast majority of children want to please their teacher, so always acknowledge positive behaviour: *'This group is working well together'*; *'I like the way you are sharing equipment'*. Build positive relationships with each child; make sure that you show that you like and respect the child, although you may not approve of their behaviours at times.

Identify flashpoints and challenging times, then be prepared to explicitly teach the behaviour that is required. For example, if lining up for assembly is an issue:

- decide on the behaviours you want to see;
- teach them to the children;
- practise until they are routine.

When the children demonstrate a required behaviour, acknowledge it and praise them for it. Establish an agreed reward system that can be used to reinforce classroom behaviours as well as to reward good work.

There are times when a child's behaviour must be addressed and consequences applied and there is a need for the child to move away from the rest of the class to calm down and think about what they are doing. Time Out procedures and dens could be considered.

Time Out systems

These can be useful in schools, as they allow a child the chance to calm down or regain control of their behaviour. They can also allow a teacher to take back control of a situation and remove the audience from a child's inappropriate behaviour. However, they need to be thought about very carefully and not used as a knee-jerk reaction or a way of removing a child from the classroom.

- **Where?** A Time Out space should be either just outside or in the corner of a classroom, for example in a 'den' (see below). It should not have too many distractions and should be able to be supervised and have access to a clock or timer.
- **How long?** Time Out should only be for a limited amount of time. Children should be given a limited number of times when they can choose to use Time Out. Otherwise you could lose them all day! Teachers should also be able to tell a child to take Time Out.

The procedure for a child having Time Out must be agreed and understood by all parties. You can use cards or tokens that are handed to the teacher, or have a system of signing on a board. The teacher needs to be aware that a child is having Time Out, and when the child returns a process should be put in place so that the child can discuss the difficulty and then be able to continue with their work.

A record should be kept of when Time Out is used and in what context. This can then be used to inform any future IEP or behaviour plan.

Dens

Dens can be used in the classroom as a safe place for a child to go when they need to calm down. Some children can have sensory overload in the classroom and need a quiet place to get back on track while feeling safe. A den can be just a corner of a classroom with curtains, or a pop-up tent in a quieter area of the classroom, or even under a table covered with fabric and furnished with a cushion or two and perhaps a soft toy. It could be a set area outside a classroom that pupils can go to or an area outdoors, such as a willow dome.

Establish a routine for ending a work session

The end-of-work sessions are particularly stressful for the BESD child, who finds managing change problematic. Your chosen routine or practice will need to be taught and understood by both children and support staff. Examples include:

- Two-minute warning: *'We have two minutes left before we pack up'*;
- Time's up statement: *'It's time to stop, so finish your word/sentence/maths question/picture'*;
- Tidy up instruction: *'Put your books/equipment in a tidy pile on the table'*;
- Preparation for moving on: *'Show me you are ready'*.

Acknowledge and reinforce through praise when the class has completed the end-of-session routine and is ready to move on.

Strategies for developing an emotionally literate class

Teach the children to talk about their concerns and feelings, especially in regard to work and relationships with other children and adults. You may need to teach children vocabulary beyond *happy/sad/angry/excited*. Always link the words to pictures, events, stories, facial expressions and body language as well as to any physical actions or sensations linked to the emotion.

Support children in openly discussing relationships and difficulties, including managing to tolerate each other in class and finding work hard.

Quality Circle Time

Quality Circle Time (QCT) is a democratic and creative approach used to consider a wide range of issues affecting the whole school community. It can be used to help children learn and understand the consequences of their behaviour and begin to take on responsibility for themselves and their immediate and wider community. This has been shown to gradually shift responsibility for inappropriate behaviour in schools from the teacher to the children themselves.

QCT has at its heart a class meeting, which involves the whole class sitting in a circle to talk about issues relating to personal, social, moral and health education. Its aims are to encourage the development of positive relationships, self-discipline, conflict resolution, assertive communication and democratic group processes alongside the skills of speaking, listening, observing, thinking and concentrating. QCT follows a clear structure:

Opening game

Round table This gives everybody a chance to speak. It is this section of Circle Time where scripted sentences are often used. For example, '*I find it easiest to work in class when …*', '*I get fed up when…*', '*I was pleased with myself when…*'.

Open forum An open discussion time which can be used to talk about and solve problems and set targets.

Celebration of successes A chance for pupils to thank others, both children and adults, for acts of kindness and so on during the past week.

Closing game

The structure is designed to build a sense of class community and the teacher acts as a non-authoritarian facilitator, encouraging co-operation and creating a climate of emotional security. Further information about Circle Time and QCT can be found in the work and books of Jenny Mosley, such as *Quality Circle Time in the Primary Classroom* (LDA, 1996).

Social Stories™

Social Stories™ were created by Carol Gray to support children with autism, but they work well to explain appropriate behaviours and responses to any BESD child. A Social Story is used to describe a social situation and to establish expectations of words or actions to use in that situation. Social Stories should be brief, positive and clear (see www.thegraycenter.org/social-stories for more information and examples of Social Stories). This is a good method of helping children reflect on difficulties in their behaviour in an indirect and non-personal way.

Establishing social skills groups

Encourage a child with BESD to develop the skills to make friends by building a small group (no more than the child plus three others) around them. It is very important that the other children provide good role models and can support the child in transferring skills learnt outside the context of the group.

The content of the programme should be shared with other school staff and the child's parents/carers so that they too can reinforce the child's social learning.

The first few sessions will need to address communication skills, which will be rehearsed as a foundation for building friendships. Each session should start with a review of skills learnt in the previous one, with the children encouraged to think of examples, since last time, of how they have applied what they learned.

Alison Schroeder has produced books and games to support social skills programmes, for example, her *Time to Talk* book and game for ages 4–8 (LDA) and *Socially Speaking* book and game for ages 7–12 (LDA).

A whole-school approach

Whole-school techniques for dealing with challenging behaviour could include the following:

Active listening

Active listening is the skill of listening 'beyond the words' to the full meaning that the child is trying to convey. Being an active listener takes practice, because it makes demands on your time, concentration and patience. However, it is an invaluable tool in supporting BESD children. These are the five key elements.

1. **Pay attention:**
    - look at the child directly;
    - focus on the child's body language as much as their verbal language.

2. **Show that you're interested:**
    - make eye contact, nod occasionally, smile and look encouraging;
    - use conversation fillers such as '*I know*', and '*uh ha*' to encourage the child to continue.

3. **Give feedback:**
    - reflect back what the child has said using phrases such as, '*So you're saying that ...*', '*I think that I understand ...*', which also acts as a valuable summarising technique;
    - ask questions to clarify unclear points.

4. **Don't be judgemental ... yet:**
    - do not interrupt – allow the child to finish what they are saying;
    - do not offer other views or opinions.

5. **Consider your response:**
    - show respect for the child, while being as honest as you can be about their behaviour;
    - acknowledge effort from the child in sharing their feelings.

For more information try http://powertochange.com/students/people/listen.

Circle of Friends

This technique is linked to Quality Circle Time (see page 33).

A group of six to eight children volunteer to support the BESD child. The group has a weekly meeting during which they play games, discuss successes and problems from the week, give feedback as to targets set in the previous meeting and set new targets for the next meeting. Between meetings, the volunteers are expected to model and encourage positive behaviour, without taking responsibility for the BESD child's behaviours.

Circle of Friends has been very successful in many schools, not only in helping BESD children to take responsibility for their behaviour but also in improving their social skills and building strong links between all children in the circle. See www.autism.org.uk for more information.

Comic strip conversations

This is another initiative from Carol Gray (www.thegraycenter.org). As a behaviour management tool, comic strip conversations are a useful way of helping children to draw events that they cannot communicate verbally. Children need to be taught the technique when they are feeling calm, but they can then learn to use colour and stick figures to represent their views about an event.

Many schools use comic strip conversations as a way of giving angry children the opportunity to draw their version of events leading up to an incident. A supportive adult helps the child to talk through their experience as they draw, and can then use the drawing, or sequence of drawings, to explore what went wrong and what can be done differently another time to solve the problem.

See www.autism.org.uk or www.thegraycenter.org for more information.

Restorative Justice

Restorative Justice (RJ) is a powerful tool that can help children of all ages to understand the consequences of their actions on others, but you will need an external Professional Development provider to introduce this, preferably to all staff as part of a whole-school approach. RJ can evoke strong emotions and feelings, so it must be done with care – it can cause damage if done badly.

All behaviour is communication, and RJ allows the communication to be heard. RJ is a way of repairing the harm that is caused by inappropriate behaviours, through bringing together those involved to discuss and talk through the issues that led to their conflict. The process provides a structure that allows communication and enables people to take responsibility for the impact of their behaviour on others.

Strategies for effective ways of working with parents

The most effective relationships happen when parents and school work in partnership to support the child.

As a teacher of a BESD child, you are very likely to need to speak to parents about the child's behaviour in class. Always bear in mind that the way that you interact with parents is a key factor in the child's success in the classroom. The key relationship in school is the triangle between parent, child and teacher. The child needs to know that there is a high level of approval and support between parents and school and any problems and challenges the child faces will be discussed and resolved in a positive way between these key adults.

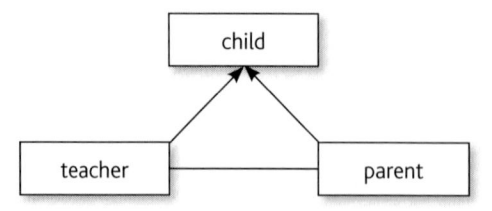

Fig. 4: The parent, child, teacher triangle.

When working with parents, bear in mind the following points.

- Treat parents with respect and try not to respond to any real or perceived lack of respect from parents. This may come from uncertainty, anger or frustration on their part, rather than being directed at you personally.
- Understand that all parents have their child's interest at heart, but they may not share the school's focus on achievement at school. Many parents say that they want their children to be happy and are reluctant to address behavioural issues, either at home or school, until it becomes absolutely necessary.
- Develop a positive working relationship with the parents and only give negative feedback after you have given positive feedback.
- Talk enthusiastically about the child; parents are very sensitive to criticism of the child, which can be viewed as criticism of their own parenting ability.
- Use metaphors when talking about the child, for example, Jekyll and Hyde. *'He is a lovely, kind boy usually, but sometimes turns into Mr Hyde and lets himself down'*. Then you can describe the unwanted behaviour before moving on to finding solutions to help the child together.
- Consider using a text messaging service to aid communications with parents; short, positive and regular messages can be very effective.
- Listen to parents and enable them to tell the story of their child; they may still be affected by the birth, difficult early years or illnesses that may have left them feeling anxious.
- Parents may feel isolated and feel that they are the only ones to have a difficult child; reassure them that they are not the only ones and that you can help the child move forward together.
- Explain why you are expecting a child to behave in a certain way.
- Be willing to admit if you have made a mistake.
- Be non-judgemental; remember that teachers and parents have different roles in the child's life. As a teacher, you will be part of a child's life for a short time, but you can have a lasting effect.
- Maintain a focus on education and avoid real or perceived criticism of the parents' life choices.
- Be honest, not critical.

The BESD-friendly classroom

A learner-friendly classroom is good for all children, especially those with BESD. The following checklist is divided into sections containing suggestions for particular aspects of classroom management, the curriculum and the school day. Different suggestions will be appropriate for different age groups and children. Some of the ideas will be right for your situation, whereas there will be good reasons why others are less suitable for you. You should take from this list only what is relevant for the learners in your classroom and for you.

Dealing with challenging behaviour and non-compliance

- Use a calm voice. Do not shout or become shrill; many children with BESD respond to the tone of voice, rather than the words that are used.
- Repeat directions and instructions using positive, repetitive language, for example, *'Jason, I need you to ...'*.
- Focus on the desired behaviour. Do not get drawn into secondary behaviours.
- Use proximity praise (comment on the positive behaviour of others in the classroom). For example, *'The Blue group are cooperating really well'*.
- Be aware of body language. Standing to the side of a child is more effective than standing close or facing them; do not tower over a child, as this can be perceived as threatening and may elicit a negative response.
- Remind children of class rules, for example, *'In our class, we speak politely at all times'*.
- Thank children for positive responses and reinforce desired behaviours when they happen: *'Thank you for lining up so well'*; *'I like the way the Blue group is working together'*.
- Use the school Behaviour Policy and request help when needed from colleagues, senior staff and SENCos.
- Make use of advice from websites such as www.behaviour2learn.co.uk which have archives of government publications relating to improving behaviour.

Creating a positive learning experience

- Offer structured, small-steps teaching with over-learning built in.
- Make learning active, with positive feedback and focused praise and a variety of activities.

- Show, don't just tell. Make maximum use of ICT.
- Create an exciting, multi-sensory teaching environment. Use images, diagrams, flowcharts, colours, mind maps, sounds, tactile objects and include active, problem-solving approaches.
- Seat children so that you can check discreetly if they have understood, and you can pick up on non-verbal communication if they are struggling.
- Organise groups so that children can support each other; do not put all the 'behavioural problems' in one group with a TA. This will lead to over-dependence.
- Give clear indicators of time left.
- Explain clearly that time will be given to finish tasks at a later point.
- Be patient and repeat directions several times, using the same language (some children need more processing time than others).
- Ensure that the classroom is peaceful and free from distractions.

Giving instructions

- Keep instructions short and clear, and repeat them if necessary.
- Provide visual support if needed.
- Break down longer instructions into smaller chunks and give children time to complete one 'chunk' before you set the next.
- Use consistent language when giving instructions.
- Check that children have understood instructions.

Whole-class teaching sessions

- Ensure that the support staff know the work that is to be covered.
- Always give the big picture – an overview of a lesson at the beginning, and a summary at the end.
- Make expectations very clear.
- Explain and check for understanding.
- Have the topic, keywords, date and day available on a whiteboard or a card on the table for dyslexic learners.
- Repeat key words and phrases.
- Allow for individual thinking time or discussion with a partner before bringing the subject back to the whole class.
- Have high, but attainable, and consistent expectations.
- Keep to the point.
- Be enthusiastic.
- Encourage children to ask questions.
- Provide opportunities for children to show creative thinking and learning. Be prepared to recognise and reward creativity in approaches and solutions to problems as well as through drama, music and so on. But do not allow children to become over-controlling.
- Always use the same vocabulary when giving directions.

Planning and organisation (for older children)

- Give children colour-coded timetables, where the colour coding aids organisation skills.
- Teach examples of planning strategies, for example, concept maps, flowcharts, timelines.
- Give written homework instructions.
- Provide age-appropriate timetables; remember that some older children dislike, or have 'grown out of', visual timetables.
- Show how to plan work or revision.

Listening

- Slow down your speech and make sentence structures simple.
- Give plenty of time to practise listening.
- Give children thinking and take-up time.
- Allow time for processing – children may need extra time to think through what has been said.
- Vary the pitch, tone and speed of your delivery to keep the children engaged.
- Check that the child has understood. Children should not be allowed to become dependent on their friends for information.

Comprehension

- Encourage children to use a highlighter pen on worksheets/tests to identify key words/concepts in a comprehension activity.
- Highlight and discuss new subject vocabulary.
- Use visual cues to support reading.
- Check understanding through discussion, asking the child to present the information in a different way, using role-play and so on.

Maths

- Teach children how to use support materials.
- Put number work into practical contexts. Use games and a variety of apparatus.
- Display an analogue and digital clock side by side for reinforcement. The digital clock is easier to read, but does not help the child understand time.

Positive reinforcement

- Allow access to a variety of ways of recording and presenting knowledge.
- Recognise and reinforce strengths.
- Carefully differentiate learning tasks without over-reliance on worksheets.
- Change groupings to avoid over-dependence and to encourage children to be flexible in their approach both to work and to peers.
- Praise work for effort and content as well as accuracy.
- Consider seating arrangements and promote peer support.
- Give clear recognition of effort.

FAQs

In this section we address a number of questions that are raised again and again by teachers of children with BESD. We hope the list of questions and answers below will help to provide practical solutions and also reassure you that other teachers and other schools face similar challenges.

Q How do I advise a parent who approaches me about managing their child's difficult behaviour at home?

A Ask the parent to briefly describe the behaviours that concern them before fixing an appointment to see them after school. Find out how the child's behaviour differs from that which you see at school and make a note of the differences. This information will help you to decide which advice to offer and where to go for further advice if needed. Remember, many children exhibit different behaviours at home and school and simple reassurance may be all that is needed.

- Ask if the child has spoken of any concerns at school or with friendships. Also, are there problems with sibling relationships/jealousy?
- Provide basic, common-sense advice regarding the benefits of a good diet/sleep/time for relaxation and of limited access to electronic games/tv in bedrooms.
- If the behaviours described seem dangerous and/or are causing physical or emotional damage to the child and/or other family members, consult the member of staff responsible for Safeguarding and explore possibilities of contacting external agencies to provide additional support in the home for the parents.
- If the behaviours cause the parent to find the child difficult to manage because of inconsistencies in their approach to parenting, then advise establishing house rules and routines (bedtimes are often a source of concern) mirroring the structure provided by school.

Q A child with BESD in my class is becoming anxious about transferring to secondary school. How can I support the child?

A Enlist the help of the parent/carer in establishing if the child has specific concerns or is anxious about the change in general.

- Discuss your concerns with the SENCo and senior leadership at an early stage, as there may be a need to liaise more regularly with the secondary school at whole-school level.
- Prepare the child by discussing aspects of the transition in the summer term before transfer. The whole class, groups or the individual child may benefit from this approach.

- Provide the child with an opportunity to express their feelings and concerns, in a group or one-to-one with you or another adult, especially after any transfer days or activities.
- Liaise closely with the receiving school and use any transfer material if available. Make sure the anxious child is in a class with other children who know them.
- Some children may wish to put together a pupil passport (see page 55) which documents what they would like staff in the new school to be aware of: personal information; preferences such as having a quiet place to be during lunchtimes; learning styles; likes and dislikes.
- Make sure the child's needs are discussed by each school's SENCos if they are on a record of support. If the child is on the Autistic Spectrum or remains particularly anxious, arrange additional visits for them accompanied by a trusted adult, during which they are permitted to take photographs, be introduced to key staff and navigate the school. Compiling a scrapbook, which can be referred to with parents during the holidays, or designing a Powerpoint presentation to be shown to classmates, provides a focus for the visits.
- Arrange for the child to be met by a designated pupil mentor or buddy who can help them settle in once the new term starts.

Q A child in my class, who has always seemed compliant, is now behaving in a challenging way. When I asked what was wrong, the child would not answer. What shall I do?

A Talk to the parents/carers as soon as possible, expressing your concern and offering support. Explain that your motivation for contacting them is because the current behaviour is out of character.

- If this is inconclusive and the behaviour continues, monitor the child closely and record behaviour incidences using the 'A, B, C' method (see page 28). Follow your school's Behaviour Policy.
- Look at friendship groups. Is this a problem?
- Is the child having difficulties with the work set, or is there evidence of bullying in the classroom or playground? Ask all staff for their observations, especially the midday staff.
- Praise positive behaviours but continue to provide opportunities for the child to express their feelings or offer reasons for the negative behaviours. They may find it easier to talk to another adult. Keep senior leaders and parents/carers informed. If the challenging behaviour continues or escalates, seek the advice of the member of staff responsible for Safeguarding with a view to taking further action and engaging external agencies.

Q What do I do if a child is isolated and appears to have no friends?

A A child new to the school may find social integration particularly difficult because they are joining a year group with established friendship groups. Utilise existing systems of support that involve responsible pupils, such as 'playground buddies'. The parents/carers, if new to the area, may also be experiencing isolation and may welcome being introduced to other parents of pupils in the same year group. Out-of-school relationships may then form to ease the child's isolation in school.

- Provide regular opportunities for collaborative work in class with different groupings, in a variety of subjects, so that all children can learn to work with others, not just their friends. This will avoid isolation and enable a range of relationships to be formed.
- Use PSHE lessons for the class to find out about each other (even a well-established class has more things to find out) and use group work so the child is included in activities.
- Social skills are vital for success in life and the parents/carers of a child who is experiencing persistent difficulties will need to be aware of your concern and intention to intervene. Their support is vital. Ask questions such as: *'Does the child have access to out-of-school activities?'*; *'Do they have friends visiting the house?'*; *'How do they spend time out of school – does the family spend time together?'* Sometimes parents/carers lack a social network and the confidence to teach their child how to socialise.

Q A BESD child has difficulty sitting on the carpet and on a chair and self-exits. What strategies should I use?

A If a child has difficulty adhering to basic classroom rules and routines, they need reminding. Establish a 'meet and greet' at the beginning of the day by asking the parent/carer to bring the child to school a little earlier; explain that this is to 'set the scene' for the day by setting some time aside for a member of staff to restate the school's expectations to the child.

- Couple this strategy with some positive recognition around the behaviours of concern: *'I'm so pleased that you sat nicely on your carpet square, Tommy'*. If the behaviours persist, develop a target card linked to a reward system. Break the targets into small achievable steps.
- If the child has a diagnosis of ADHD they may be taking medication, which is reviewed regularly. Make sure you are fully cognisant of routines around the medication plan and keep parents/carers informed about any concerns about behaviour. Be mindful that schools are expected, by law, to make reasonable adjustments for children with disabilities and all school staff must have had training in the management of a child with ADHD. Consult the SENCo for further information.
- Keep parents/carers fully informed and on board by using a home-school book to record the child's achievements against targets. Keep comments positive and use other means of communication to deliver any negative reports about behaviour that you think parents/carers need to know.

Q The parents of a BESD child in my class are reluctant to be involved with or have regular contact with the school. How may I encourage contact?

A Some parents/carers have bad memories of their own schooling. Others may think that home and school are separate worlds and that it is the school's role only to educate. A parent/carer may be wary that a teacher wishing to speak to them must be about to deliver bad news about their child's behaviour and seek to avoid contact.

- Start by communicating positive comments as well as concerns about behaviour. Don't just send Molly home with a piece of work labelled 'Well done'; 'speak' directly to parents/carers. You can phone, text, write a postcard or send an email saying that you *'really want to tell them…'*. It may take time to build trust.

- Meet the children at the door or in the playground and make a point of speaking to the parents in a friendly way, showing that you have a positive relationship with their child; this will make it easier to discuss any challenging behaviour at a later date.

- Have an Open Morning or Time After School where children can bring in their parents to show them what they have achieved. This does not have to be formal and can lead to parents not seeing school as a threat.

- Some parents may lack the confidence to become involved and may need encouragement. If your school welcomes parent/helpers, the starting point may be to ask for their help to support you.

Q Some parents are complaining that their children are being bullied by a particular child, in and out of school, although I have no evidence of this. Should I respond?

A If a parent requests a meeting to discuss this issue, revisit your school's Bullying Policy beforehand so you are clear how you are expected to respond. The parent is entitled to a copy of the policy if they wish. See parents individually, not in groups. Make sure a senior member of staff or headteacher is involved and a note is kept about matters discussed.

- However reticent a child may be to report an incident of bullying, they will need to speak to you, with a parent/carer present if they wish. See potential 'witnesses' individually and offer the children the opportunity to write their accounts of any experience they may have had or witnessed in school. Ask the midday staff to observe the children's relationships and behaviour during lunchtime play so that you can get a clear idea of what is actually happening and then make a plan to deal with the problem.

- Focus on the 'bully' and find out if there is any reason for the child's behaviour. It may also be useful to speak to the parents of this child to see if they know of the behaviour and if you can work together to help the child change the way they relate to other children. You may need to have support from a senior member of staff, but aiming for a partnership/no blame approach will make the meeting more positive.

- Emphasise that, in order for the school to deal with bullying, children need to speak to school staff as soon as possible.

- Speak to senior leaders about any issues of staff deployment if you think extra vigilance is advisable. Request that the school's attitude and approach to bullying forms the basis of an assembly or class work in PSHE.

Q How do I motivate a child who tries to avoid work by distracting tasks such as extended pencil-sharpening, or by comments such as '*This is boring*'?

A Check that you have differentiated the work appropriately and the pupil understands the task they have to do.

- Make time outside of work time for pencil-sharpening.
- Make it clear to the class what you expect from them on a task-by-task basis.
- If the child has not achieved what you think they are capable of, or delays beginning work, use sanctions such as losing minutes of break time. Make sure that these are used fairly and the whole class understands that this is the consequence for wasting time.

- Set a short-term target for the individual child with a clear reward when the target is met.
- Notice and comment on compliance: *'You should be proud of yourself, Dean, for writing those sentences in the time set'*.
- Ignore dismissive comments or be unmoved. Try telling your class that dealing with boredom is an important life skill.

Q How do I encourage my TA to support a child appropriately, as the child is dependent on her?

A TAs need to be informed about the teacher's intentions and, if written lesson plans are used, provided with plans in advance.

- Plan for yourself and your TA to work with all children during the week, to discourage individual children from seeing the TA as being there for them alone.
- If a dependence has developed, take immediate steps to encourage independence. This may need to be considered very carefully if the TA has been assigned to work with the child as a key worker due to a specific need or attachment issues. Make sure that you work with SEN children/groups, as well as the TA.
- Talk to colleagues who taught the child in previous years so that you are fully informed of the child's history. Ask the TA to consider ways in which the child can move forward, as the TA knows them so well. Consult your SENCo about putting together a plan.

Q I have a child in my class who incites others to misbehave. How do I address this?

A Check that you have differentiated the work appropriately and that everyone understands what they have to do.

- Keep a note of when this behaviour happens and look for a possible pattern. Does it occur before lunch, after play, when the child is asked to write something? The behaviour could be masking an underlying difficulty.
- In class sit the child under your nose, away from their friends, and micro-manage their every move until realisation dawns that every infraction of rules has an immediate consequence – a principle which should form the basis of your classroom management of all the children. Notice and recognise effort and compliance, using descriptive praise as outlined on page 91.
- In the playground, find the time to observe the child's interactions with others and consider, with the SENCo, the possibility of including the child in a social skills group. Include midday supervisors in this.

Q How do I try to modify the language of a child who hears swearing at home and uses it at school?

A Remind everyone at first and then the child in a one-to-one situation of expected behaviour in school and state that inappropriate language is not acceptable. Younger children may not realise, until told, that certain words are unacceptable.

- Ensure you include 'use of appropriate language' as a part of the class rules which you set at the start of the year. Then you can remind the child that *'we don't use that word in our class'* by pointing to the agreed class rules, which are displayed on the wall and referred to at regular intervals with everyone.

- Check the school's Behaviour Policy so you can quote it. Your task is made easier if there is already mention of how 'bad/inappropriate' language is viewed and dealt with in the policy (which should be accessible to all parents) or included in your classroom rules (which should be displayed at the start of the academic year).
- In principle, it is irrelevant that the child hears swearing at home, as they have to learn that it is unacceptable in school. Enlist the support of a senior leader, especially if the child swears routinely. Ask to see the parents/carers and the child with the senior leader and explain your concern, referring to the Behaviour Policy, to demonstrate that the child is breaking a rule rather than causing offence to you personally. Work in partnership with the parents to support their child.
- Some senior leaders may advocate zero tolerance; some may take a more tolerant approach and use a daily monitoring report which aims to focus the child on reducing instances of swearing and rewarding them if they succeed. The child could be asked to take the report to the leader each afternoon at the end of school. Ideally this would be as the parent/carer collects the child.

Q How can I encourage a child to show respect for all staff members, not just teachers?

A It goes without saying that, in order to tackle this issue, staff must model respect for each other. It helps if all staff address each other by their surnames in front of the children.

- It is helpful if the class can see the teacher and TA as a team, so they know they will get the same response from both adults.
- In a small community children may know members of staff socially or as family members – which can confuse younger children, who may be used to calling Mrs Smith, your TA, 'Cheryl' out of school. It is an issue worth raising with parents/carers, as an off-the-cuff comment about Cheryl's personal life may undermine the professional standing of 'Mrs Smith' in school.
- Make it clear that all adults who work in school are deserving of the same level of respect. All adults should reinforce this message, both informally as needed and more formally in assemblies or PSHE lessons.
- The key is to coach staff to respond to incidences of disrespect in a neutral way using the *'You are breaking a rule'* mantra rather than a more personal *'I'm not going to stand for that!'* type of response, however offended they may feel. With rule-breaking, a reminder of expected behaviour and an automatic consequence should follow.

Q What do I do about a child who is aggressive towards peers and staff?

A Act swiftly, as someone could get hurt and the child could face exclusion. The child needs a planned programme of support involving the parents/carers and a senior leader to steer the process. Inform a senior leader that you wish to talk to the parents/carers in their presence.

- Find out the reasons for this behaviour. Talk to previous teachers/other staff and – importantly – to the child. Make sure that the child knows that their behaviour is unacceptable and they are breaking a very serious school rule/expectation.

- Your programme needs to incorporate a pupil risk assessment, a behaviour management plan and at least three targets for the child, broken down into achievable steps. Try to work out what the child is trying to tell you by their behaviours. Are they masking a learning difficulty? All staff must be aware of, and involved with, the programme in order to reinforce expectations and reward the child's successes as they occur. The programme should be reviewed by the senior leader and you with the child and parents/carers every two weeks, face to face. The child's successes can be celebrated at these meetings when targets are achieved and modified.
- Consult your SENCo when drawing up documents and alert the member of staff responsible for Safeguarding.

Q How do I respond when a child steals?

A If you are certain that the child took the item, stay calm and talk to the child to give them the opportunity to explain themselves. If possible, have a witness present and record events.

- If you are uncertain, announce to the class that something is missing and provide the opportunity for it to be replaced: *'Jane's watch is missing. Everyone search the classroom please'*.
- Stealing can be a symptom of complex issues. A very young child, on the other hand, simply may not understand the concept of ownership. Be vigilant and discuss your concerns with colleagues, especially those who have previously taught the child or may know the family well. A useful article on this topic by Leah Davies can be found at: www.kellybear.com/TeacherArticles/TeacherTip65.html.

Q What strategies do I use when a child persists in shouting out instead of raising their hand?

A Begin days/lessons/tasks with an activity that reminds the children of your expectations of conduct. You may have used such activities at the beginning of the year to settle your class. Even with older children, never assume they will automatically conform to expectations, as a group, unless you have taken the time to teach them. This can be done in a fun and lightweight way; it is a more effective way to manage than constantly reminding the individual child.

- Let's assume you have a rule, such as: *'We put our hands up ... We don't shout out'* displayed on a card, with a picture of someone holding their hand up. Tell the children to close their eyes and put up their hands if they can remember a class rule without looking. Take some time to discuss reasons for rules.
- If the child still persists in shouting out, praise them on the occasions that they do raise their hand and ignore them if they do not: *'Well done Lulu, I saw you start to raise your hand instead of opening your mouth to speak – I'm very pleased with you'*.

Q If a child is withdrawn and seems unhappy, how should I approach them?

A If this is out of character, approach the child directly and ask them if they would like to speak to you or another adult on their own, as you are concerned about them. Make sure you adhere to your school's Safeguarding Policy with regard to possible disclosures.

- Speak to colleagues who have taught the child and may know the family to find out if the child usually presents in this way. If the family has experienced upheaval, such as a divorce or bereavement, the child's behaviour may be a response to trauma and/or loss. Refer to the relevant person in your school to investigate the availability of further support, such as counselling services, in your locality. Speak to parents/carers about your concerns, as they will need to make the approach to an out-of-school service.

- A shy child may lack the social skills to make friends and may benefit from intervention. Speak to parents/carers about encouraging the child to participate in activities out of school and pair them up in class, for some tasks, with a peer who is a good role model.
- Observe the child in class/in the playground and, if they seem over-anxious and/or fearful, consult the member of staff responsible for Safeguarding.

Q How do I respond to a child who says *'I'm stupid'* when asked to address tasks?

A Ask why they say it, because you know it is not so. If 'friends' or family have said this to the child, tackle this by speaking to parents/carers or other children individually. Comments like these have a corrosive effect on a child's self-esteem and need to stop.

- Develop a positive ethos in your class, in which everyone feels valued for themselves and knows that if they cannot succeed at first, then they will succeed later if they try hard and ask for help when needed. All attempts are part of the learning process: encourage a 'can do' attitude and help children learn that in order to succeed, they have to fail a few times first. Use examples: *'You had to learn to crawl before you could walk'*.
- If family members are not encouraging the child, give advice and demonstrate how this can be done, by instituting a home-school book which notes how you recognise achievement and good conduct: *'Marlon was very helpful to me today by giving out the painting trays ... he achieved a determination sticker for completing difficult sums'*. Make sure the book is signed at home and similar comments are added by family members.
- Encourage participation in out-of-school activities.
- Notice and recognise every small step of progress the child makes – and check that the work is differentiated appropriately.

Q What do I do with a child who refuses to attempt work?

A If the work is differentiated appropriately, the child understands what they are expected to do and you are sure it is within the child's capabilities, be relentless.

- Start by using a timer, as outlined on page 89. Be clear in your expectations and seat the child away from any distractions. Break the task down into chunks and give a time for each part. Do not allow the child to go out to play until they have completed what you set them to do. (Make sure that this is not the reason for the child refusing to work – to some children, one-to-one time with the teacher is preferable to playtime.) Enlist the support of a senior leader but do not allow the child to go to the leader's office or sit in a corridor to do their work, as their place is in your classroom under your management. You may experience major inconvenience to yourself with this strategy for a short period, but once work starts to be produced (and praised to the skies!) it will be worth it.

The Target Ladders

Aspect 1: Coping in the classroom

Letter	Interacting with adults	Readiness for learning	Skills for independence	Getting attention appropriately
A	Answers simple questions from teacher/trusted adult	With support, sits on the carpet area with other children	Separates from parent/carer to another adult	Looks in the direction of the adult speaking
A	Asks simple questions of teacher/trusted adult (e.g. 'When is it playtime?')	Sits on carpet area and listens to instructions	Separates from parent/carer and goes into school unsupported	Responds to adult speaking and showing them attention (e.g. will smile in response to a smile)
B	With support, begins to tell an adult what they did outside school	Sits on carpet area and responds to instructions	Hangs coat/bag up in the morning	Begins to follow others and puts hand up to talk to teacher on carpet
B	Starts a conversation with trusted adult about what they did outside school	Sits on carpet area and puts hand up to answer questions	Hangs coat/bag up in the morning and goes into classroom	Puts hand up when answering questions
C	Works with an adult to complete a task	Sits at a table to work with a known adult	With support, will move around the classroom as directed	Works alongside other pupils with an adult (e.g. around a table)
C	Follows an instruction from an adult to complete a task	Sits at a table and works with any adult	Moves around the classroom as directed	Sits at a table with others independently
D	With support, tells an adult if something has happened	Through questioning, talks about what they are doing	Moves around the classroom to different chosen activities	Knows the names of children and adults in class
D	Tells an adult as soon as something happens	Talks about what they are doing	Moves around the classroom to different directed activities	Knows the names of all children and adults and uses them correctly

The Target Ladders

© *Target Ladders: BESD*   LDA   Permission to Photocopy

Suggested activities or strategies

Note: All children start school with a different set of experiences. Some will have attended nursery and be familiar with start-of-the-day routines. Others may not understand what lining up means and have difficulty with the idea of personal space, or even following someone else. Establish expectations (this can be turned into a game). Pictures of the sequence of what they need to do could be used as a reminder; give praise and rewards when children get it right. Establish the morning routine with parents/carers so that they support their child's independence.

Classroom routines

When children first arrive at school, everything will be unfamiliar. Name cards and badges for adults and pupils can help children familiarise themselves with what the name looks like. These can be used for sorting games or finding-your-place games to help everyone settle. Those who cannot read can look at their badge and find the name card that looks the same.

- Have a timetable of activities (pictures and words) so that children can refer to it if they are unsure. If you are using pictures, attach Velcro or magnetic tape to the back so that they can be moved when the activity is finished or to build in change.
- Label areas and resources in the classroom.
- Always refer to what is happening next. A large number of children like to know what is happening before moving on to each lesson.
- Make sure that everyone understands classroom rules and routines. If necessary, break them down into a sequence of tasks. For example, lining up: break down the sequence of actions and skills needed so that no misunderstandings arise. Practise routines and make them into a game to establish them; for example, practise lining up by numbers or in alphabetical order of names or by eye colour.
- Prepare for change so that children gain the skills needed to face the unexpected.
- Make sure all adults are known to the children. Message games, in which the children have to go to different adults to get different bits of information, can help.

Forming relationships

Trusting relationships are the foundation of all work with children with BESD.

- Meet and greet the child each morning.

An identified and consistent adult should:
- look for the child's arrival into the school building each morning;
- greet the child enthusiastically;
- support them with any routines for taking off their coats and so on;
- take them to do an individual and enjoyable activity.

During the activity, the adult should help the child to unburden themselves of anything that has happened before school and help the child into a mood in which they are receptive to the day's activities.

- Once the child has established a relationship with this adult, encourage the child to go quickly to the adult as soon as anything disquieting happens. At this stage in a child's emotional development, the adult should try to sort out the problem and praise the child for seeking help.
- Encourage the child to seek out their named adult during the day if they have done something that they are proud of, too.

Learning names

- Take photographs of all of the children in the class and label them.
- If you have a 'talking pen' (see www.talkingpen.co.uk), use it to enable each child to say their name. Let different children use the talking pen to swipe the recordable dots and hear the names of the children.
- Focus your Circle Time warm-up time on games and activities that involve naming the children: for example, saying a child's name before throwing or rolling a ball to them; using blindfolds and guessing who's talking.

Aspect 1: Coping in the classroom

Letter	Interacting with adults	Readiness for learning	Skills for independence	Getting attention appropriately
E	Talks to a familiar adult about an object that interests them	Asks questions to get more knowledge about something that interests them	Knows where to go to get what they need (resources)	Takes turns in activities with adult supervision
E	Talks in front of the class about an object that interests them	Is keen to find out more about something that interests them	Is able to collect what they need	Takes turns in activities without adult support
F	Takes written messages to adults in other places in the school	Writes some sentences independently	With adult direction, will move around the school	With adult direction, will knock at a door and wait for response from adult
F	Delivers a simple verbal message to an adult	Writes some sentences independently on subject of their choice (e.g. a short story)	Moves about the school independently	Knows what to do in order to take and deliver a message
G	Contributes to class discussions when asked	With support, will begin to take part in simple problem-solving activities	Co-operates with others to complete an adult-led task	With reminders, will follow classroom rules for contributing to lessons
G	Voluntarily contributes to classroom discussions with the teacher	Attempts simple problem-solving activities with peers	Co-operates with others to complete a task with adult nearby	Knows that different lessons allow for different responses
H	Knows that talking with adults can have positive outcomes (praise) or negative outcomes (consequences)	With support, finds solutions to curriculum problems (e.g. making a bridge to hold a weight)	Collects own resources needed to solve a problem	Prefers positive to negative attention from adults
H	Seeks positive interactions with adults	Finds solutions to problems using ideas from teacher input	Sorts out own resources to solve a particular problem	Knows that negative attention-seeking behaviours have a consequence

The Target Ladders

Suggested activities or strategies

Talk time

Establish opportunities in the classroom to encourage children to talk with each other, both one-to-one and in small groups, and with all adults who work in the classroom.

- For any talking activity, guidelines and rules need to be established beforehand to stop the situation getting out of control. Rules should be discussed and agreed; everyone can sign the rules to say they will adhere to them. The consequences of not sticking to the rules should also be agreed.
- Establish protocols for talking in Circle Time activities or class discussions. Talk tickets or 'magic crystals' can be used to establish the idea that only one person at a time can speak. Interrupting a child who is talking, or talking out of turn, could lead to the interrupting child not being able to contribute for a certain time or being asked to leave the circle.
- Older children can take part in a 'cotton bud' or 'button' debate, in which each child is given a certain number of cotton buds or buttons, and they hand one in every time they talk. When they have run out, they have to listen to what the others have to say.

Praise and consequences

Help children to understand the rules in your classroom by being explicit about the behaviours for which you give praise and consequences.

- When giving praise, instead of saying, '*Well done*' or '*Good boy*', say, for example, '*Thank you for holding open the door for Mr Jay. That was very polite.*' Or '*You sat and listened for 5 minutes today. That was your target. Well done for reaching your target.*'
- When giving consequences, say, for example, '*You were asked to sit quietly in assembly. You had a warning, but you kept on making silly noises. Your consequence is that you have to go and apologise to Mrs Brown.*' Or '*The school rule is that we don't fight. The consequence for fighting is that you miss a playtime*'. When giving consequences, try, where possible, to refer to school rules in order to make it impersonal.

Building co-operation skills

Learning to play and work with peers and adults is an essential skill. Co-operation skills also build the foundation for more complex social skills. Teach children about co-operation through group activities that require waiting, turn-taking, and following directions.

- **Cooking** Small group cooking activities offer opportunities to divide work and practise skills. You could have a written or pictorial recipe with ingredients and steps presented in order. Assign roles to each child, such as measuring the flour, counting the correct number of eggs, pouring the milk, greasing the pan, and stirring. Children have to wait their turn, follow directions, and share responsibility.
- **Gardening** When potting seeds or planting flowers, children can have individual responsibilities such as digging holes, counting seeds, putting seeds in the holes, patting dirt over the seeds, and watering. Gardening also provides the opportunity for continuing co-operation and responsibility.
- **Role-play** Role-play situations that require co-operation, and discuss good choices with the children.
- **Games** Encourage children to play games and discuss issues. Board and card games can often be made into team games, which foster co-operation and team strategies.

Problem-solving

Activities that include a problem-solving element can help a child develop their own strategies, as well as help them to understand why certain decisions have been made.

- Ask the children, as a class or group, to come up with possible solutions to help with a real-life problem (for example, to stop arguments over a particular toy or activity).
- Use Circle Time to discuss class issues in a non-threatening environment.
- Have a class or school council, where children take it in turns to help come up with solutions to issues raised.

Aspect 1: Coping in the classroom

Letter	Interacting with adults	Readiness for learning	Skills for independence	Getting attention appropriately
I	Discusses their work with a teacher	Accepts that they don't always get it right	Says what is wrong	Is aware that attention needs to be shared
I	Discusses their work with a teacher and knows what needs to be done to improve	Accepts that they don't always get things right and finds a solution	Says what is wrong and what is needed to sort it out	Is aware and understands that attention is shared
J	Tells a teacher that they don't understand	Listens to further explanations in order to help understand	Works in stages in order to complete a task (chunking)	Is not distracted by others for a limited period of time
J	Explains to a teacher why they don't understand	Reacts positively to further explanation	Works unsupervised until a task is finished	Completes a task without distractions
K	Shares worries with an adult	Is prepared, with support, to try something new	With support, will accept new challenges	Takes on more responsibility in response to positive praise
K	Seeks out an appropriate adult to share worries	Is keen to try new things	Is willing to take on the challenge of new things	Is able to take responsibility positively
L	Sorts out difficulties with peers, with an adult acting as mediator	Knows that they cannot succeed all the time	Knows where to get help if it is needed	Talks about what they could do next time
L	Asks an adult to act as mediator to sort out difficulties with other children	Sees setbacks as a way of moving on	Has the resilience to know how to cope with a setback	Talks about what they could do next time and is able to act on it

52   *The Target Ladders*

© Target Ladders: BESD   LDA   Permission to Photocopy

Suggested activities or strategies

Following the rules

Play board games to reinforce the idea that the rules have to be followed and only one person can win.

- Initially, set up the board game for two people only, you and the child.
- Explain the rules, including how to win the game.
- Agree that playing the game is a fun activity and that the purpose of the activity is only to have fun.
- If you lose, congratulate the child on winning, but make more of the fact that you both shared an enjoyable activity. If you win, acknowledge that you enjoy winning, but make it clear that your main pleasure was from the shared activity.
- Once the child is able to lose to you without getting upset, ask them to suggest another child who could come and join your shared activity.

Bouncing back

Building resilience – the ability to bounce back when things go wrong – helps children manage stress, anxiety and uncertainty. Children with good self-esteem tend to be more resilient. Strategies that can help children to build resilience include the following:

- Making friends. Teach the child that the best way to make friends is to be a friend: to listen to others and show empathy for their hurts; to socialise together; to share experiences and frustrations.
- Identify the worry. Help children to identify the things that are worrying them the most. Once the worries are out in the open, encourage the child to focus on something else for a while.

Working independently

It is just as important for a child to be able to work independently as it is for them to be able to work as part of a group.

- Set clear expectations and guidelines for the finished product.
- If the process is more important than the finished product, explain the criteria and what you are particularly looking for (this may be different for different children).
- Praise those working as directed.
- If a child has difficulty in sustaining independent working, various strategies can be used to build up the time the child can work without needing adult attention, for example:
  - Break down the task into smaller achievable 'chunks'. Each chunk will need to be explained as well as the finished product. You can check each chunk as a way of making sure the pupil stays on track.
  - Use a timer. A sand or digital timer can reassure the child that an adult will be back after a certain time to check that there isn't a problem.
  - A Help Card can also be used. This can be put in a prearranged place so that the adult knows when the child needs support. A limit can be put on the number of times it can be used per session, once the method of use is established.

While establishing the idea of working independently it must be remembered that some pupils, whether or not they have a recognised difficulty, need to have movement time in order for them to settle and concentrate. This should be built into their classroom routine so as not to cause disruption and unsettle others.

Building relationships

Building good relationships is an essential part of helping a child to cope in the classroom; until a child trusts the adults around them, they are likely to reject offers of help.

- After any incident or challenge with a child a discussion should be had, when everyone has calmed, to discuss what happened and if anything could be done next time to give a different outcome.

Aspect 1: Coping in the classroom

Letter	Interacting with adults	Readiness for learning	Skills for independence	Getting attention appropriately
M	Talks to adults on a range of issues	Talks about their own strengths and weaknesses	Knows how they need to move on with their learning	Uses knowledge of strengths and weaknesses positively
M	Is comfortable talking to adults on a range of issues	Understands their own strengths and weaknesses	Knows and is able to move on with learning	Talks about strengths and weaknesses and accepts advice
N	Acts with adults appropriately in a range of situations	Knows what they need to do to be successful at secondary school	Knows what they need in order to be organised and ready at secondary school	Talks about what has helped/not helped at school
N	Talks to adults appropriately in a range of situations	Is keen to take on the challenge of moving to secondary school	Organises self to be ready for secondary school	Reflects on their time at primary school

The Target Ladders

Suggested activities or strategies

Sharing worries about moving to a new class or school

Children need access to a trusted adult, who they know gives them praise and support as well as consequences.

- Role-play cards or scenarios can be used to examine situations at a distance, so that they do not become too personal to the individual. These can be particularly useful when dealing with playtime or friendship issues, as you are only asking what advice they would give or how they would deal with a situation. These solutions can be acted out or made into posters or cartoon strip stories and used as a resource if the incidences happen in 'real life'.
- Drama can also be used to help children know how to respond appropriately to adults in new situations. Understanding about body language and how to present themselves in different situations can help all children, but is particularly useful for those who are impulsive or can be unco-operative. This can also be used as part of transition work to help children prepare for moving on to another class or school.
- Understanding their own strengths and weaknesses can also help pupils in dealing with their own particular concerns or worries. Posters about likes and dislikes, or booklets which explain what they enjoy or don't enjoy about various things, such as lessons, playtime, holidays or sports, can be useful for the class teacher and can go with older pupils to secondary school.

Reflecting

- At the end of any year it is good for children to be able to reflect on what they have enjoyed and learned. This can be done by choosing work/art/photographs that they are proud of or that remind them of something. Most schools will have a set tradition for what happens when pupils leave primary school – a Year Book, poems, assembly – where pupils can reflect on their time at school. This helps them to move on to the next phase of their education by showing how far they have come already.
- As part of this process, encourage children to consider themselves both as a learner and as a friend. Show them how to do a SWOT analysis (identifying **S**trengths, **W**eaknesses, **O**pportunities and **T**hreats) in order to identify aspects of their personality they want to develop and those they want to change.

Pupil passports

Pupil passports come in many different formats to suit children of varying ages in a range of contexts. They create the opportunity for the 'pupil voice' to be heard and give children the chance to show their strengths as well as their areas for development. This helps teachers in a new school to make relationships more quickly and successfully.

Pupil passports are a useful tool at the point of transition into secondary school, because they give the children the opportunity to record what helps them to learn, what they find hard and what support they would like to receive.

A pupil's organisational skills can be addressed and identified on a pupil passport. As part of the process, give the child the responsibility of thinking about how they can be supported in improving organisational skills (such as visual timetables, lists in their lockers and at home, reminders in homework planners).

Aspect 2: Unstructured times

Letter	Understanding social expectations	Appropriate interactions	Managing conflict	Managing the play-to-work transition
A	Knows they should look at the person who is talking	Looks briefly towards the person who is talking	Names feelings *happy*, *sad* and demonstrates awareness of what they mean	Runs around freely in the playground
A	Knows they should look at and listen to the person who is talking	Makes eye contact with the person speaking	Says what makes them *happy* or *sad*	Knows they can have fun with others in the playground
B	Knows that the rules of a board game make the game fair	Says '*please*' and '*thank you*' when prompted	Recognises when characters in stories are *happy* or *sad*	Says where you can run and shout
B	Names rules that help them, such as how to stay safe when crossing the road	Says '*please*' and '*thank you*' unprompted on occasions	Names actions in stories that make others *happy* or *sad*	Knows they can run around and shout in the playground but not in the classroom
C	Explains how playground rules keep them safe	Interacts with another person in the playground	Names feelings *excited*, *upset* and demonstrates awareness of what they mean	Knows that when play is stopped they have to go back to the classroom
C	Says why they cannot run around and be noisy in the classroom	Listens to two simple instructions in order, such as '*Pick up the ball and throw it*'	Says what makes them feel *excited*, *upset*	Stops playing when asked to by an adult
D	With adult support, follows the rules of a simple board game or playground game	Watches others play	Names actions in the playground that may make others *excited* or *upset*	With support, uses a timer to focus on an activity for 4 minutes in class or playground
D	Follows the rules of a simple board game or playground game without adult support	Says '*Can I play with you please?*' to another child	Names feelings *friendly*, *proud* and demonstrates awareness of what they mean	Accepts the end of an activity when given a minute's warning

The Target Ladders

Suggested activities and strategies

Naming feelings

Emotional literacy – knowing about feelings – is very important if children are to learn to manage their feelings in socially appropriate ways. Help the child to recognise and understand their feelings.

- Use mirrors. Ask them to make the faces they make when they are happy, sad, excited.
- Use photographs. Can the child tell you what people in the photographs are feeling? Can they suggest reasons why the person might be having that feeling? What makes them feel that way?
- Talk about the way that the face changes as emotions change. Explicitly point out to children how the position of the eyebrows, how widely open the eyes are, and the shape of the mouth, can all show how a person is feeling.
- 'Reflect' the child's feelings. If they are feeling happy/sad/cross, say to them, 'I think you're feeling happy/sad/cross because …' 'Your face looks happy/sad/cross.' 'If you are feeling happy/sad/cross, would you like to …?'
- Use stories and poems. Discuss how characters in the story are feeling and how we know that they are feeling this way.

Board games

A wide range of attractive board games is an indispensable behaviour management tool. Ensure that the games you have are relevant to the age and developmental stage of the child.

When you play a board game with the child, bear in mind the following:

- Start by establishing the rules.
- Ask the child to explain the rules to you to check that they understand the rules. Can they explain why we need rules to play a game?
- If you win the game, talk to the child about how they feel. Can they describe where in their body they are experiencing the feeling? Reflect their feelings back at them to give them words to describe the feelings.
- Discuss the idea that only one person can win a board game. Talk about what the other players get out of playing the game.

Joining in with games

Some children are isolated in the playground because they don't know how to ask if they can join a game.

- Use small world people or puppets to act out playground scenarios.
- Develop an agreed script, so that all children in the class are familiar with it. The script needs to include the following:
  - A request to join the game, such as, *'Please can I play with you?'*
  - An affirmative response, such as, *'Yes. We're playing … and the rules are …'*.
  - A negative response, such as, *'No, I'm sorry'*, together with acceptable reasons. For example, *'We have even teams but if you can find someone else then you can join in'* or *'There isn't room for anyone else to fit in the space'*.
  - Appropriate reactions, such as, *'Thank you'*, or saying *'OK'* and walking away.

Now and Next boards

Use a Now and Next board to help the child to manage transitions.

To make a Now and Next board, you need symbols, photographs or images from a visual timetable. Ideally, laminate each picture and put a Velcro dot on the back so you can reuse it. Put a Velcro strip on a piece of stiff card. Stick the relevant pictures to the Velcro strip.

- Before the child goes out to play, remind them that Now is playtime and Next it will be … (for example, literacy).
- When they come in from play, use the board to show them that Now it is … (literacy) but Next it will be an activity that the child would choose and enjoy.

Now and Next boards are very effective ways to remind children that they have to do what the adult requests before they do their chosen activity.

Aspect 2: Unstructured times

Aspect 2: Unstructured times

Letter	Understanding social expectations	Appropriate interactions	Managing conflict	Managing the play-to-work transition
E	Knows that taking part in a game is fun even if they don't win	Plays alongside another child with some interaction	Knows who to approach if they need help in the playground	Leaves an unfinished activity positively
E	Tells someone that they liked playing a board game even if they lost	Takes turns in games, with support	Has fun in the playground with friends	Returns to an unfinished activity after a period of time
F	Understands the consequences of breaking a rule (e.g. losing a minute of playtime)	Takes turns in games, without support	Names actions in the playground that may make others *friendly*, *proud*	Recognises cues that signal the approaching end of playtime (e.g. a bell)
F	Accepts a consequence (e.g. losing a minute of playtime)	Invites others to join a game	Accepts help from an adult	Is able to accept that they are not first in a line
G	Is aware that others' attention has to be shared	Asks to be included in group play in the playground	Is able to say '*sorry*', when prompted, if they upset another child	Will line up when prompted at the close of play
G	Is aware that equipment has to be shared	Responds to another child's request to share equipment	Is able to say '*sorry*' unprompted on occasions if they upset another child	Will line up unprompted as cued
H	Takes turns with equipment during activities	Requests a turn with equipment politely	Follows rules for sharing without becoming upset	Responds positively when asked to line up in a particular way
H	Understands they have to co-operate with others when playing in the playground	Listens to others' suggestions for playground games	Is able to resist the temptation to join in with unwanted behaviour	Accepts a consequence (e.g. going to the back of the line) if they do not line up as directed

The Target Ladders

Suggested activities and strategies

Talking object

To encourage the child to understand and value the concept of taking turns, use an object such as a soft toy or a decorated stone as a part of Circle Time.

- Explain to the child that the person who holds the object is having their turn to talk.
- While the person is talking, everyone else has to be quiet and listen to what is said until the object passes to another person.
- The child raises their hand if they wish to have a turn to speak and the teacher directs when this takes place.

Understanding conduct rules

The concept of school rules may need to be taught to the child. Not all children will have had experience of these types of adult-led rules.

- Begin with familiar situations in which rules keep the child safe. Discuss why rules are necessary and what may happen if there are no rules.
- Remind them about what they need to do when crossing the road. Help them break up what they do into small ordered steps, so that they create their own 'rules of the road' using a storyboard.
- Discuss the playground rules and how some keep the child safe (no climbing) and how some help the child feel safe (we don't hurt each other).

Choices and consequences

Use the language of choice to help the child manage their feelings. If they make a bad choice help them reflect on consequences.

- Encourage the child to recognise the feeling: 'You are becoming upset because ...'.
- Emphasise the need for a consequence if a rule is likely to be broken.
- Offer alternative courses of action: 'You can choose to finish the work before play or during play ...'.
- Immediate brief consequences are most effective; congratulate the child for making the right choice and avoiding the consequence.
- To help them reflect on the bad choice, explore how the consequence could have been avoided had they decided on the right course of action.
- Use role-play, puppets and stories to develop the language of reflection.

Social Stories™

The concept of Social Stories™ was developed by Carol Gray (see www.thegraycenter.org). These are short stories written, word-processed, illustrated and developed with the child to achieve a desired behaviour. The writer and protagonist is the child: illustrations can be the child's drawings or photographs. The story should be carefully presented in book form so that the teacher can use it to remind the child of the desired behaviour before an occasion, not as a consequence of a bad choice.

- Write a Social Story about lining up, or sharing playground equipment.
- Ask the child to think about when and why the class need to line up and what can happen in a line; what may the children do deliberately or accidentally?
- Encourage the child to describe the line moving in terms of safety and order.
- For how long do the children stay in the line and who leads the line?
- Discuss with the child how the teacher decides who leads the line and how the children take turns to lead.

Aspect 2: Unstructured times

Letter	Understanding social expectations	Appropriate interactions	Managing conflict	Managing the play-to-work transition
I	Identifies the playground zones in which they would like to play	Knows that they may say 'No thank you' if they do not want to play with others	Is able to say 'I would rather not play with you today'	Can wait in line without disruption
I	Plays in more than one playground zone	With support, develops own ideas of group activities	Uses more than one 'I' statement to express needs and feelings	Tells adult about a playground incident before class
J	Chooses when to join in and when to opt out of a group	Offers suggestions of activities within a group	Names feelings *angry*, *surprised*, *disappointed*, *scared* and demonstrates understanding of what they mean	Accepts that some things have to be resolved later
J	Understands that others have different ways of doing things	Appropriately offers opinions about group activities to others in the group	Remains calm when others in a group become involved in conflict	Understands that entering the school building is entering the learning zone
K	Plays co-operatively when others alter the rules	Makes positive comments about others, such as complimenting peers on their ball skills	Recognises triggers for conflict, such as when other children shout at each other	Walks along corridors to class observing the rules
K	Is willing to alter the rules themselves to improve or vary the game	Accepts positive comments about themselves	Seeks help at the point at which conflict can be avoided	Enters the classroom in the way the rules dictate
L	Is aware that they may suggest playground games to others	Invites others to join them in playground activities	Understands that others have different views	Recalls a previous instruction, about the task, given before play
L	Takes a leading role when playing a game in the playground with others	Invites others' compliance during play through demonstrating a skill or role (e.g. 'You can do it like this ...')	Uses 'I' statements to express their views and opinions	Shows enthusiasm for classroom-based activities

60 *The Target Ladders*

Suggested activities and strategies

'I' statements

Teach the child to manage their responses by using 'I' statements to express feelings and wishes, replacing 'You ...' or 'Don't ...' at the beginning of a sentence. Communicating in this way helps to defuse potential arguments, because the child is stating how they feel, not making accusations or issuing commands. Teach them to always start the sentence with 'I', say how they feel and state the action which caused them to feel that way.

- In the classroom the child says '*I want you to ask before you borrow my pencil*' instead of '*Don't take my pencil*' or '*You can't take my pencil*'.
- In the playground the child says '*I felt upset when you shouted at me*' instead of '*Don't shout at me*'. Or, '*I don't like it when you call me names*', and so on.

The child should also be taught to use 'I' statements to encourage understanding of how others feel: '*I can see that you are cross*'.

Positive 'post-playtimes'

Establish a short Circle Time session (see page 33) at the beginning of afternoon lessons, to recap on the lunch break in a positive way.

- All children can only comment on positive actions.
- The child can think of a game that has gone well.
- The child can say how a compliment made them feel.
- The child can suggest how another child was helpful and kind or demonstrated self-control.

A useful resource for Circle Time is *Turn Your School Round* by Jenny Mosley (LDA).

Playground friends

Establish a system of 'playground friends'. These are children whose responsibility it is to play with other children who are feeling left out and lonely and help the others to find games they can join in with.

- Encourage all children to be playground friends at some time.
- Do not make being a playground friend dependent on good behaviour: it should be an expectation that all children will take the role for a short time if they are willing to do so.

Keep calm and carry on

Reassure the child that feeling angry and upset sometimes is OK. Teach strategies to help them express and manage their emotions when experiencing anger. They will need to be taught these when they are calm and responsive.

Encourage them to think of ways in which they could manage this feeling of anger and stay in control of their actions.

Supplement the child's suggestions with simple strategies:

- Counting backwards from 10 under their breath.
- Relaxing their body by breathing in for five counts and out for seven.
- Dropping their shoulders to relieve tension.
- Removing themselves from the place or person that is upsetting them.
- Finding someone else to talk to or play with.
- Self-talk, such as '*I'm feeling calm and fine*', repeated under their breath.
- Turning to an activity that they enjoy and which helps them calm down, such as reading a magazine, kicking a ball, playing with LEGO®.

Becoming positive

Encourage a positive 'can do' attitude among all children in the class. This is important, both for a child's self-esteem and for establishing an understanding that being miserable does not command more adult attention than being positive.

- Expect to hear a positive comment before you listen to any complaints or negative comments.
- Ask children to tell you what they do know, as well as what they do not know, when they ask for help.
- Give all children a feeling of ownership and responsibility for their learning by giving them options wherever possible.

Aspect 2: Unstructured times

Aspect 2: Unstructured times

Letter	Understanding social expectations	Appropriate interactions	Managing conflict	Managing the play-to-work transition
M	Identifies others with whom they share common interests	Identifies potential friends	Accepts that friends can upset each other sometimes	Leaves playground arguments in the playground
M	Explores friendship with a wider range of peers	Has some strategies for making friends	Does not bear grudges	Is accepting of where they are told to sit and with whom
N	Is confident and comfortable in the playground, whether or not with friends	Is welcoming to newcomers	Understands that restorative approaches can prevent further conflict	Co-operates with peers and staff without distraction
N	Volunteers for a position of social responsibility	Helps newcomers integrate socially	Engages in restorative approaches	Responds to verbal or non-verbal cues from the teacher that signal readiness for learning

Suggested activities and strategies

Taking part in group work

During all group work activities, give children experience of taking all roles in a group: from chairing and managing the group, to reporting back on decisions made by the group.

Talk together about how to successfully manage a group – or how to take a leading role in a game. Make sure that children know that the leader doesn't always have to take all the decisions, but they do have to understand them.

Make explicit links between these activities and games in the playground. Explore ideas together such as the following:

- Should the same person always be the leader?
- Does the leader have the right to tell others what to do?
- What happens if someone disagrees with the leader?
- Is the leader the only person who can decide whether someone else can join in the game?

Making and breaking friends

Explore the idea of 'friend' with the whole class.

- What does 'friend' mean?
- What do you do with a friend?
- How do you make a friend?
- How do friends relate to each other?
- How do you know if someone will be your friend?
- What happens when friends disagree?
- How do you make friends when you move into an established group or class?

The more you can talk about these ideas openly together, the more you can support all of the children in understanding how they make and break friends.

Principles of Restorative Justice

'Restorative Justice' (see page 35) is most powerful when practised as part of the whole-school Behaviour Policy. The basic difference between restorative and retributive justice is that in restorative justice, the culprit has to face up to how they made the victim feel and take responsibility for the inappropriate behaviour. Both children agree a contract about their future behaviour towards each other and the culprit's apology is generally more heartfelt and may be accompanied by some appropriate action to make amends.

Even if there isn't a whole-school policy about Restorative Justice, you can explore with the class how much of the principle you want to absorb into your own class.

Signals for learning

Older children can often recognise fairly subtle signals that it's time to work independently and co-operatively. However, it is still useful to have some kind of agreed visual or verbal sign of your expectations. These might include:

- A 'noise-ometer' which shows children your expectation regarding classroom noise levels. Should they work in silence, or can they speak quietly, or talk normally, or use playground voices?
- A symbol to indicate whether children should be working independently, in pairs or in groups.

The more 'visible' you can make your expectations, the better the child's chances of meeting them.

Aspect 2: Unstructured times

Aspect 3: Controlling emotions

Letter	Recognising feelings	Developing control	Understanding effects of actions	Communicating needs
A	Can name feelings *happy, sad*	Shows by facial expression when they are *happy* or *sad*	Shows an awareness of what *happy, sad* mean	Says that they are *happy, sad*
A	Can say when they are *happy, sad*	Says when they are *happy* or *sad*	Says what makes them *happy, sad*	Says why they are *happy, sad*
B	Can name feelings *happy, sad, angry, OK*	Can recognise feelings in people in photographs/pictures	Knows when others are feeling *happy, sad*	Can say that others look *happy, sad*
B	Can name and identify feelings *happy, sad, angry, OK*	Can identify when they are feeling *happy, sad, angry, OK*	Begins to recognise a reaction in others when they show their feelings	Can ask others how they feel
C	Knows that a feeling causes a reaction (e.g. people cry when they are sad)	Knows what makes them feel better when they are *sad*	Knows they can cause a feeling in others	Says what they need to make them feel better when feeling sad or upset, from a choice of options
C	Can link a feeling to an event	Knows that doing something will make them feel differently	Knows they can cause a feeling in others and make it change	Says what they need and acts on it
D	Can say when they have felt *happy, sad, angry*	Is beginning to understand that doing something can make them feel different	Links feelings to actions	Knows what will make them angry, before they get angry
D	Can say when they were *happy, sad, angry* and explain what it felt like in their body	Links events to a particular feeling	Begins to grasp the idea that an action may change how they are feeling (e.g. looking at a book may make them feel less angry)	Can say what will make them feel calmer, before they get angry

The Target Ladders

© Target Ladders: BESD   LDA   Permission to Photocopy

Suggested activities or strategies

Talking about feelings

There is a wealth of activities and stories that can be used to help children begin to recognise and name feelings.

- Use photographs as a sorting game. Children can sort them into *happy, sad, angry* or identify which picture would look like them if a particular event had happened (for example, if they had a day out at a park, or if someone had spoilt their game).
- Play 'Feelings Snap' with laminated pictures or pre-bought cards.
- Cut out pictures from newspapers/magazines and make *happy, sad, angry* posters.
- Play 'Guess the Feeling' – children can act out a feeling for others to guess. You can suggest prepared scenarios or pupils can act out something that makes them feel *happy, sad* or *angry*.
- Make paper plate faces showing different emotions.
- Have a feelings wall or interactive display in the classroom where the child can put a picture of themselves showing how they are feeling. The picture can be changed throughout the day or for different activities.
- Choose words that children have to say in ways that express different emotions. For example, say '*sausages*' in a *happy, sad* or *angry* way.

Recognising feelings in pictures or photographs

- A large picture or photograph of a person (or group of people) can be used to prompt a discussion about how the person is feeling. How do we know? How does seeing this make the children feel?
- A collection of different photos or pictures – holiday photos, animals, patterns, and so on – can be used as a starter to PSHE lessons. Individuals choose a picture that makes them feel happy/sad/calm and so on, and – if they can – say why. Calm/happy pictures can then be used when the child is feeling upset or angry, as a way of talking about contrasting feelings.

Knowing what makes you feel better

Talking with children about how things make them feel is the first step to teaching them to self-calm.

- Look at photographs of events in school, or talk about events at home. How did those events make them feel?
- Look at objects with different features and textures – sparkly, soft, tactile and so on – as well as books and pictures. Ask children which object, picture or book makes them feel calm or happy when they handle or touch it. Suggest that the child might choose that object next time they are becoming angry and see whether it still makes them feel calm or happy.

There are also structured stories such as the one in *Forest of Feelings* by Carol Holliday and Jo Browning Wroe (LDA), which can be used as part of a programme of study.

Recognising body signals

As we begin to get angry, when the brain is not yet flooded with adrenaline, there are physical signs which warn us that we are getting angry.

Help the child to think about their own signs. Common ones include:

- feeling hot;
- feeling a burst of energy;
- clenching fists;
- grinding teeth.

Help the child to understand that the feeling of anger is allowed … but that they need to control how they show their anger. Before they can control it, however, they need to recognise it.

Once they know they're getting angry, help the child to develop a list of things they can do to calm down, such as:

- taking themselves away to a quiet place;
- lying down and focusing on breathing deeply by raising and lowering their tummy (put a toy on their stomachs so that they can see it going up and down);
- running in an agreed place;
- repeating a positive, self-calming mantra: '*I can calm myself down*'.

Aspect 3: Controlling emotions

Letter	Recognising feelings	Developing control	Understanding effects of actions	Communicating needs
E	Acknowledges that feelings can be positive or negative	Knows that there are feelings within the range of *happy*, *sad*, *angry*	Sees that different feelings promote different reactions	Begins to identify what is needed to change how they are feeling
E	Understands that it is OK to have negative feelings	Knows that they have feelings within the range of *happy*, *sad*, *angry* and begins to be able to show where they are on a feelings thermometer	Notices how their body changes with different feelings	Explains how they can change what happens within them when they are feeling negative (e.g. using exercise instead of wanting to hit out)
F	Communicates when they are feeling negative	Recognises feelings associated with disappointment or frustration	Knows that the body changes when experiencing negative feelings	Explores ways to change a negative feeling
F	Communicates verbally when feeling negative (instead of through behaviour)	Understands feelings associated with disappointment	Knows how their body changes when experiencing negative feelings	Knows what helps them when they are feeling negative
G	Knows that all feelings are OK	Knows what a feeling looks like to them	Knows effects of feelings on themselves	Talks about what happens to them in a variety of feelings
G	Knows that awareness of their own feelings allows them to make a choice	Knows what happens to them in a variety of feelings	Knows effects of feelings on themself and others	Talks about what happens to them and others in a variety of feelings
H	Names a full range of feelings	Matches a feeling to a picture or description and names it	Says when they had a particular feeling	Listens to ideas about how to change a negative feeling
H	Names a full range of feelings and knows what it means to feel them	Sorts feelings into categories	Says when they might have a particular feeling	Offers own ideas to change a negative feeling

The Target Ladders

Suggested activities or strategies

Where do you feel it?

- As part of a PSHE lesson, children can prepare help sheets for others describing how to deal with things when they are feeling negative. For example: *'If you are feeling angry you could ... count to ten slowly, go and look at a calming picture'*. These sheets could be displayed on a wall so they can be referred to and added to as appropriate. This helps to show children that everyone can have negative feelings, but what matters is how they deal with them.
- Try giving the children outlines of bodies, on which they can mark which bits of their body change when they feel certain emotions. For example, the head feels lighter when they are happy; there is tightness in the stomach or fingers get hot when they are getting angry.

Exercise and relaxation

- Use relaxation time, so that children know what it's like to feel calm. You can play music or use a relaxation story. However, remember that individuals may have different ways of calming down, and what may soothe one may annoy another.
- Exercise, and how we feel before and after exercise, can also be a good way to introduce the idea of what happens to our body when we are feeling in a certain way. Some children like to run or climb when they are upset, and recognising this and incorporating those activities into other lessons can help to normalise behaviour and help the child begin to understand why doing something helps them when they are feeling bad.
- Use Circle Time to have discussions about how we react to different situations, so that children begin to understand that all feelings are OK, but the important thing is how you deal with them.

Using feelings thermometers

Feelings thermometers can be useful to allow children to gauge how they are feeling and also for them to reflect afterwards on how they calmed down. Generally, high numbers suggest negative emotions and low numbers are calm/happy.

- 'Thermometers' are simple scales which can take on different forms or shapes depending on how they are going to be used in the classroom. A simple version that works well is 'happy face to sad face' along a line. Alternatively, use 'happy face to angry face' with a calm face in the middle. Thermometers or rockets can be used for display purposes.

Sorting feelings

Talk about the feelings words in the table below. Children can discuss what the word means to them (word association) and when they might feel like that. Some words will need adult explanation, as some children will confuse emotions (especially negative ones) in an effort to explain them.

Positive feeling words	Negative feeling words	Other feeling words
happy	angry	shy
joyful	anxious	silly
loving	afraid	curious
cheerful	sad	embarrassed
excited	grumpy	tired
proud	annoyed	exhausted
content	jealous	lonely
pleased	guilty	bored
delighted	worried	confused
enthusiastic	frightened	nervous
motivated	scared	surprised

- Sort feelings words into positive (make you feel good) and negative (make you feel not so good) feelings. Different feelings can be given colours, or pictures, chosen by the children, to help them. This can then be used to help children talk about negative feelings to others.
- Find 'feelings synonyms' or 'feelings opposites' to help to refine understanding of feelings words.
- Make Lotto games in which you ask the children to match feelings words with feelings pictures, symbols or photographs.

Aspect 3: Controlling emotions

Aspect 3: Controlling emotions

Letter	Recognising feelings	Developing control	Understanding effects of actions	Communicating needs
I	Knows that other people have feelings and emotions	Begins to read social situations – body language and so on	Knows that we have choices in how we act	Names feelings in others
I	Can tell if other people are feeling different emotions	Reads different situations and can read body language	Makes choices about actions	Names and understands feelings in others
J	Understands that feelings are natural, but that they have to control their responses	Knows it is OK to have different feelings	Can feel when they are starting to have a negative feeling	Tells others when they are getting upset
J	Understands that feelings are natural, but that they have to control their actions	Knows it is OK to be angry, but not OK to throw things or hit someone when angry	Knows when they are beginning to get angry	Explains to others what they need to do to help when getting angry
K	Knows that some things hurt their feelings	Knows that feeling hurt causes a reaction	Knows the effect of others' feelings	Says, *'You are hurting my feelings'*
K	Lists the things that hurt their feelings	Knows what happens to them when they feel hurt	Understands the effect of others' feelings on self	Knows what to do when someone hurts their feelings
L	Knows some things to do when feeling negative	Knows what helps when they are feeling a particular emotion	Knows how to manage their feelings in a positive way	Talks about a variety of ways to make themself feel differently (self-calms)
L	Knows which actions will enhance or diminish feelings	Knows what helps when they are feeling a particular emotion, and acts accordingly	Knows how to manage their feelings in a positive and safe way	Acts on the way that makes them feel differently (self-calms)

The Target Ladders

Suggested activities or strategies

Saying 'You've hurt my feelings'

Telling others how they make you feel is a skill which is frequently modelled in American cartoons and TV soaps.

- Talk about why it's hard to say how you feel.
- Use puppets and small world toys to develop scripts for sharing the information.
- Create scenarios for children to explore, using and adapting the scripts.
- Emphasise that the child has a right not to have their feelings hurt, but they have a responsibility to share the information politely and calmly.

Dealing with conflict

Encouraging children to talk about events, both positive and negative, helps them to build their emotional intelligence and become more self-aware.

- When something has happened, the child talks it through with an adult one-to-one, and works out what could be done differently next time. When doing this, it is important for the adult to recognise the feelings involved, and help the child to understand that it is OK to have those feelings.
- Complete an incident form or a reflection form or draw a picture of what happened.
- Everyone involved talks the incident through.
- Restorative Justice (see page 35).

Self-awareness

As a child grows and develops, they recognise their own likes and dislikes and understand what makes them the same as, and different from, other children. This helps raise children's self-esteem, as they learn that they are individuals who have worth, just as they are.

- To help a child learn more about themselves, make posters of all the things they like. They could include favourite food, pop stars or football players and use pictures cut out of magazines or downloaded from the internet. Older children could use presentation software on the computer to create something similar, which could be added to throughout the year.

- Have special times when children compliment the others in the class. Teachers will need to make sure everyone is included.
- Giving responsibility teaches a child about their capability. Responsibilities also help raise a child's self-esteem, when they find that they are able to accomplish various tasks.
- Children also need to be aware of their responsibilities and how they are different from an adult's responsibilities. They need to understand that allowing them to make small decisions is the first step to being more responsible.
- Within school, responsibilities can range from classroom monitor to school council representative, depending on the capabilities and confidence of the child. All children should be given the opportunity to have a responsibility – a hidden talent may be discovered.
- Community projects help children to see that they can be valued and make a worthwhile contribution locally. Such projects can include helping to plant flowers or tidy up a local area, or can extend to involving local authorities if there is something that they feel needs to be changed, or if there is an amenity that they feel the council needs to provide.

Positive thinking

One of the most powerful ways of self-calming is by being positive. Help children to identify things to make themselves feel better.

- Identify a daydream which can be returned to and which is positive and happy (such as winning a match, or being in a calm place) or plan a positive experience.
- Think about how someone you like and admire would deal with the situation.
- Find someone to help you.
- Find someone you can help.
- Run around the playground. This is an ideal way to 'let off steam' to enable a positive mindset on returning to the classroom.
- Talk to yourself using positive language: *'I can control my temper'*; *'I can do this'*.

Aspect 3: Controlling emotions

Aspect 3: Controlling emotions

Letter	Recognising feelings	Developing control	Understanding effects of actions	Communicating needs
M	With support, can control their emotions and show confidence in age-appropriate social situations	Is starting to use self-knowledge to help them cope in age-appropriate social situations	Knows what to do to manage their feelings around others	Begins to control how they are feeling around others
M	Can control their emotions and show confidence in age-appropriate social situations	Uses strategies to overcome feelings in age-appropriate social situations	Can appropriately manage their feelings around others	Behaves appropriately in situations involving different people
N	Is beginning to feel confident enough to say how they feel in a range of age-appropriate situations	Begins to be in control through self-knowledge	Begins to react appropriately to others	Begins to accept who they are in relationships with others
N	Can confidently say how they feel in a range of age-appropriate situations	Can be in control through self-knowledge	Reacts appropriately to others	Accepts who they are in relationships with others

Suggested activities or strategies

Building relationships

Help children build healthy relationships with others.

- Encourage children to work with someone they have not worked with before.
- Ensure that adults model good relationships with each other.
- Give children the chance to have free and frank discussions about their relationships with their peers.
- Support children in making friendships with peers who have similar interests in music, clothing, cars, sports, and so on.

Learning respect

- Model respect for other people's feelings and property. Role-play cards or scenarios can be used to reinforce the idea of respect and how others feel when not shown respect. Older children can look at and discuss relevant newspaper articles.
- All children will need boundaries and eventually will have to make them part of their lives. Classroom rules and a whole-school code of conduct will help children understand boundaries, but children will be more willing to accept those boundaries if they are part of the decision-making process. Parents should also be encouraged to be part of this process.
- Respect other points of view. No relationship is without conflict in one form or another, and compromise is a key ingredient in maintaining good, healthy relationships. Where good relations are concerned, winning isn't everything. Modelling and encouraging children to say how they feel in certain situations helps them to be more open in their relationships and gives them the confidence to cope, when they are older, when they are uncomfortable in a relationship.
- Be a good role model. Our children spend many unsupervised hours away from home, and inevitably they leave the family. Learning how to choose good friends and how to nurture friendships is an important part of growing up. These skills can make coping with life's hardships a lot easier when they occur.

Building social confidence

Confidence, in children, comes from feeling good about themselves and having healthy self-esteem.

- Help children to understand their own strengths and weaknesses and feel good about themselves.
- Teach the skills to deal positively with different social situations as well as the resilience to deal with setbacks when they arise. Talking about films and photo-stories, and using role-play, puppets and small world toys are particularly useful techniques for this.
- Realistic praise and positive reinforcement from an early age help to develop confidence, as well as the understanding that mistakes are learning opportunities, not major failures. Be aware that false or unrealistic praise can reinforce children's negative feelings about themselves.
- Phrase your comments so that advice is given positively, and not seen as criticism. This should be part of good practice.

Aspect 4: Taking responsibility

Letter	Developing ability to take responsibility	Developing self-knowledge	Reflection	Accepting consequences
A	With support, starts to tidy up after self (e.g. picks up toys)	Begins to make choices modelled by an adult	Works and talks about what they are doing with an adult	Understands the need to pick toys up
A	Puts one toy away before choosing the next activity	Makes choices and follows simple instructions	Says why they need to pick up toys	Realises the need to put things away before having something else
B	Hangs coat up, changes shoes and so on	Knows that they can do certain tasks independently	With support, asks for things or says if something is lost	Understands that if they don't do something, it may not be done
B	Organises belongings (e.g. on arrival at school)	Knows that they need to organise self (e.g. pack their school bag to go home)	Says where belongings are	Is able to tell adult if they have forgotten something
C	Does age-appropriate jobs, if modelled by an adult	Works alongside others to develop skills and independence	Talks about what they have done	Realises that things will not always go as they want
C	Does age-appropriate jobs, if modelled by another child	Knows that they can do tasks by themselves	Explains to others what they can do	Knows that they need to tell someone if things are not OK
D	Will begin to say or begin to be able to draw what happened in an incident or dispute	Attempts tasks they have not attempted before	Explains to others what happened	Is able to listen to others question their version of events
D	Talks about or draws their version of events	Finds best way to say or draw what happened	Explains to others what happened and begins to think about why	Realises that others may have their own version of events

The Target Ladders

Suggested activities or strategies

Modelling roles and responsibilities

Teaching a child to take responsibility for themselves is an essential process to enable them to maintain relationships and trust. Learning takes place through modelling, instruction and reflecting on experiences. Having consistent rules and boundaries that children understand is also important.

- Make putting toys away, or necessary routines such as hanging up a coat, into a game. For example, use a timer to see how many toys can be put in the box in 1 minute, or make a counting game so everyone picks up five things.
- Use 'backwards chaining'. You do most of the activity, but encourage the child to finish it, in order that they feel successful. For example, you help the child to put on their coat and begin to do the zip up, but enable them to complete that movement. Gradually expect them to start the activity at an earlier and earlier point, until they are completing the entire activity independently.
- If the child consistently has difficulty in completing the task, breaking routines down into stages helps to make clear where the difficulty is.
- Younger children also benefit from picture instructions so that they can see what to do next. For example, if coats are taken off before entering the classroom, then put photographs on the classroom door of children without coats entering the classroom.
- It is important to be consistent when modelling the behaviour you want to see, as some children will follow what an adult is doing. An adult hanging their coat up near the children's, or helping to clear away, will reinforce the message.
- Including parents or carers in helping to establish and reinforce routines will give the child consistency, and can help parents establish similar routines at home.

Take the time

In a busy classroom, it it often easy to jump to conclusions about a child's motives as well as their actions. Children's trust in adults is shaken if they feel that they are not heard and that they get into trouble all the time even when they didn't mean it.

- Make time to talk to the child about what happened.
- Allow them to draw, role-play or tell you what they intended to happen.
- Instead of asking '*Why did you ...?*', ask:
  - What did you **want** to happen?
  - Is that **what** happened?
  - **Why** did it not happen?
  - **What** will you do differently next time?

Incident resolution

Some children find it difficult to talk about something that has happened, or sometimes they are too emotional.

- Getting them to draw what happened (it could be stick people) gives a concrete base to start a conversation. This also allows for the emotion to be taken away from the situation.
- If all involved are able to draw/write what happened, it gives a fuller understanding to the adult involved in any incident resolution or Restorative Justice work. This also helps the child see that there could be more than one version of events.
- When getting a child to draw an event, it is best to start with one picture of how it ended. With practice they can then draw back from the end result until a series of pictures is drawn.
- Once the idea of recording incidences is established, children can draw/write the sequence of events as a flow diagram. This can then be used to show where a different action at a particular time could have produced a different result.
- An important part of this process is deciding how the child can put things right, and making sure this putting-right action (for example, an apology, or an act of restoration) is carried out in order to bring closure to the incident.

Aspect 4: Taking responsibility

Letter	Developing ability to take responsibility	Developing self-knowledge	Reflection	Accepting consequences
E	Talks honestly about events involving others	Knows there is a need to be honest	Thinks about what has happened	Realises that something will happen to them as a result of an event (a consequence)
E	Will be honest in talking about events involving self	Understands the need to be honest	Thinks about what has happened and questions others' versions	Realises that consequences also happen to others
F	Accepts praise for being honest	Knows that not being honest has a consequence	Talks about why they need to be honest	Knows that not being honest has risks
F	Begins to see reasons for telling the truth	Understands why not being honest has a consequence	Understands that not being honest makes different things happen	Sees that being caught not being honest will trigger a negative event
G	Says if something is unfair for self	Tells someone if they think something is wrong	Talks about how they see things	Listens to others' points of view
G	Says if something is unfair for others	Has the confidence to talk to a range of people	Talks about how others may see things	Understands that others' points of view can lead to a different outcome
H	With supervision/ modelling, carries out age-appropriate activities (e.g. helps tidy an area of the classroom)	Sees that as an individual they are important	Makes choices as to how something is done	Knows that sometimes they can make the wrong choices
H	Works independently in age-related activities	Understands that they are important and have self-worth	Understands that choices can be good or bad	Understands that a different choice will make different things happen

74   *The Target Ladders*

© *Target Ladders: BESD*   LDA   Permission to Photocopy

Suggested activities or strategies

Being honest

- Teaching a child to be honest is best done by modelling the behaviour you want to see. If a child sees adults owning up to their mistakes, they will understand that owning up is a consequence of making that mistake.
- Praise and reward for being honest is important, as is a consequence for not being honest.
- Consequences do not have to be severe, but they do have to be consistently given.
- Stories can also be used to teach about the importance of being honest. For example, 'The Boy Who Cried Wolf' (Aesop's fable).
- Role-play cards can be used to give examples of situations, so that children can talk about and reflect on how they would behave in various circumstances.
- You can also use continuum lines across the floor of the classroom – where children stand to show how strongly they agree/disagree with an action – to promote a discussion on what they would do in certain situations.

'Star of the week'

There are many different ways of celebrating individual children in a class. This is one.

- Put up a photograph of your 'Star'. Ask each child to say, write or draw something nice about the Star: what they're good at, what kind of person they are, something kind they once did, and so on.
- Invite your Star and a friend to make a display showing their strengths.
- In Circle Time, leave the space on the left of your Star vacant.
  - Ask your Star to invite someone to sit next to them and to give a reason (for example, *'Please come and sit on my left because you helped me with my sums'*).
  - The child to the right of the new empty seat should now invite someone else to sit there (for example, *'Please come and sit on my left because you let me come to your party'*).

Either stop the game after five children, or continue until all of the children have been named.

Giving responsibilities

Giving a child an age-appropriate responsibility or job helps to promote trust, give self-confidence and build self-worth.

- Although discreet supervision is important, give the child the opportunity to complete the task independently, otherwise they will not feel trusted.
- Responsibilities could reflect a child's strengths or be used to give confidence to someone who struggles in a certain areas. For example, the task of keeping a chart of when birthdays are in the class could be given equally to someone who enjoys making lists as well as someone who struggles with numbers.
- Try to make sure that all children get the opportunity to have some form of responsibility throughout the year. Some recognition of their responsibility, such as a picture on a display board, reminds children of what they can achieve.

Making choices

Understanding about making choices is important for children in order for them to become independent. Younger children should only be given an either/or choice (*'You can either read a book, or do a jigsaw'*) whereas older children can have several options. It should be explained that once they have made their choice, that is a decision.

Choices in the classroom can be (for example) the type of game to play, what colour paper to use to write on, or what topping to put on a cake or pizza in cooking. Older children can follow adventure games, in which the choice they make leads to different actions happening in a story.

Aspect 4: Taking responsibility

Aspect 4: Taking responsibility

Letter	Developing ability to take responsibility	Developing self-knowledge	Reflection	Accepting consequences
I	Understands the need for consequences	Understands the need for rules	Knows why we have rules	Knows that breaking rules has a negative consequence
I	Accepts the consequences in proportion to an action	Knows they need to admit when they are wrong	Sees that admitting when they are wrong is a good choice	Accepts that there will be a negative consequence to breaking a rule
J	Gets on with others in a small group	Knows that they have a role within a group (belonging)	Politely questions others' points of views	Knows that questioning a point of view will have an effect on others
J	Understands the rules of working with others	Understands turn-taking when working co-operatively in a group activity	Says when something is unfair	Is sensitive in questioning others' points of view
K	Is able to co-operate with others	Begins to develop skills of give-and-take	Thinks about others' points of view	Accepts others' points of view
K	With adult support, can reflect on times when they were unable to co-operate	Works independently within a small group	Includes others	Accepts others' points of view and reaches a compromise
L	Develops lasting friendships	Knows who they get on with and why	Interacts appropriately with different people	Knows that friendships have positive and negative outcomes
L	Takes responsibility for being a friend	Knows what makes themselves and others a good friend	Tolerates a range of people	Gets involved in activities with others

The Target Ladders

Suggested activities or strategies

Consequences

Just as children need praise and rewards for doing things right, they also need to understand that all actions have consequences.

- Consequences can be positive or negative and should be well-established and agreed within the whole-school Behaviour Policy.
- Children need to be reminded of the rules and consequences frequently and adults need to make sure all children know what they mean.
- Ensure that children understand that their choices are their own responsibility, so peer pressure and *Because he told me to* will not reduce any consequences.
- Negative consequences should be proportionate and fair. It is not the severity of the consequence, but the knowledge that it will happen, that is the deterrent for most children.
- Positive consequences should include specific praise and be in public.
- It is important that all consequences are consistently followed through.

Friendships

PSHE lessons are a good opportunity to develop the idea of friendship and to reflect on what makes a good friend. There are a lot of PSHE resources available on friendships, including SEAL resources.

- Opportunities to talk about what makes a good friend and to disentangle friendship issues occur on a daily basis and should be used as learning opportunities.
- Draw round hands and cut out the hand shapes. Children's qualities can be written on the fingers. These can then be used to make friendship wreaths or circles for display.
- Make concertina chains of people out of paper (concertina the paper and cut out figure shapes so they are holding hands). Qualities can then be written on them.
- Use co-operation/finding out activities to develop friendships within the classroom. For example, make a 'Bitsa'. Put the children in groups of six, and give each child a part of the body to draw round on someone else. These 'bits' are then cut out and decorated. Working co-operatively the children then re-make a whole body using the bits they have cut out – a 'Bitsa'. Each Bitsa is then given its own name by the group and it is put up as a display.

Reflection

Invite children to reflect on their behaviour, their interactions with others, their strengths and areas for improvement.

- PSHE lessons are a good time to discuss and reflect on events.
- Rules and guidelines need to be established. Older children are able to discuss rules and why we have them, and transfer skills taught to the wider context of social situations.
- Encourage children to keep reflection logs. These can be picture-based (using smiling to sad faces) with younger children. The purpose is to get the children to reflect on how an event, lesson or situation went for them. A diary or reflective journal can be introduced for older children. These can either be discussed one-to-one or in a group, depending on the situation.

Aspect 4: Taking responsibility

Letter	Developing ability to take responsibility	Developing self-knowledge	Reflection	Accepting consequences
M	Is confident in some age-appropriate social situations	Makes good behaviour choices in some situations	Begins to think about how they need to behave in different situations	Begins to see benefits of different behaviours in different situations
M	Is confident in most age-appropriate social situations	Makes good behaviour choices in most situations	Acts on how they think they should behave in different social situations	Repeats behaviours in subsequent situations to get same effect
N	Begins to think about differences in self and others	Begins to see differences in self and others as positive attributes	Begins to reflect how differences in self and others affect social interactions	Begins to accept themselves for who they are
N	Confidently says what they are good at/less good at	Sees differences in self and others as positive attributes	Is able to reflect on how differences affect social interactions	Accepts themselves for who they are

Suggested activities or strategies

Social situations

In the classroom it is important to nurture the child's social skills as well as their academic ability.

- Adults should act as good role models for developing skills and set the tone for appropriate behaviour in the classroom.
- With younger children, set up a role-play area to practise specific social skills in a certain situations – for example, taking tea with the Queen. With older children, use drama/ literacy lessons to role-play a situation such as complaining in a shop, or booking a holiday, in order to promote a discussion about how we talk to others in different situations. Different events could be added to show that different people affect the outcome.
- This could be developed further into situations such as job interviews, or set up a television or radio channel where the pupils have to present a piece about themselves giving their strengths and weaknesses. This could be recorded and used for future discussions.
- Helping to plan and organise an activity for everyone, such as a garden party or barbeque, will help put skills learnt into practice and also give children confidence in their own abilities.

Same and different

Play a game to help children think about sameness and difference.

- Put children into pairs.
- Give each pair a grid that has two columns: Same and Different. The grid should have a number of rows with headings such as:
  - **looks** (same and different in height, eye colour, skin colour, hair colour etc);
  - **likes** (same and different in tastes in food, music, TV, sports etc);
  - **actions** (same and different activities, leisure activities);
  - **reactions** (same and different feelings and responses).
- Ask each pair of children to think about themselves as a pair and write at least one thing that is the same and one that is different about themselves in each cell.

Self-confidence

For a child to be self-confident they must:

- know that they are believed in;
- understand that they are a worthwhile individual;
- be reassured that it is OK to make mistakes;
- know they will be actively and reflectively listened to;
- have their feelings acknowledged;
- know that it is their behaviour that may be criticised not them;
- have their fears and anxieties accepted as genuine;
- have their independence encouraged;
- have their successes celebrated;
- be laughed with not at.

This list is adapted from the BBC Health website www.bbc.co.uk/health/physical_health/child_ development (see the section on Emotional development: Building confidence in children).

Once a child is confident in their own ability they are able to see strengths in others and difficulties that others face, and have empathy for them.

- Team-building or problem-solving games help children see each other's strengths.
- Working in groups, in which each child has a role, also promotes seeing each other in a positive light.
- Philosophy for children can also be used to develop enquiry skills and to develop children's confidence. Each child can discover their own strengths and realise that they don't always have to be right for their ideas to be of value. They will also gain opportunities to help others to develop their ideas.

Aspect 5: Social interactions with peers

Letter	Sharing/taking turns	Working as part of a group	Friendship skills	Dealing with disputes
A	Passes an object to and fro (e.g. rolls a ball to an adult)	Works alongside another child without interaction	Plays alongside another child for 2 minutes without interaction	Names feelings *happy*, *sad* and demonstrates awareness of what they mean
A	Passes an object to and fro (e.g. rolls a ball to another child)	Makes a comment such as *'Look, I've drawn a cat'* to a child working close by	Makes brief eye contact when addressed by another child	Says to another child what makes them feel *happy* or *sad*, as directed by the teacher
B	Says *'My turn, your turn'* when rolling a ball back and forth	With support, asks another child to pass them something (e.g. a piece of equipment)	Shows something, such as their comfort toy from home, to another child without letting it go	Listens briefly to another child telling them about their feelings around *happy* or *sad* things
B	Identifies where characters in stories are sharing something	Asks another child to pass them something (e.g. a piece of equipment)	Lets another child briefly touch a treasured object	Through role-play, demonstrates understanding of a link between a feeling and an action
C	Through role-play, demonstrates understanding of how characters in a story share something	Passes a piece of equipment to another child at their request	With support, interacts with another child in the playground	Says if a character is *kind* or feeling *cross* in a familiar story
C	Understands that if they wish to share a toy they have to ask first	Follows classroom routines for working where in the room the teacher directs	Briefly interacts with another child in the playground	Says what makes them feel *cross* to another child (e.g. in Circle Time)
D	Shares an activity by taking turns with another child (e.g. placing pieces of a small jigsaw)	Uses language such as *'We had to work together to do/make this ...'*	Watches others play	Listens, in Circle Time, to another child describing when they feel *cross*
D	Takes turns, with one other person, according to the rules of a simple board game or playground game	Takes turns, in a group of three, at placing pieces of a medium-sized jigsaw	Asks if they can join in a small group having fun in the playground	Says what they like and dislike doing

The Target Ladders

Suggested activities or strategies

Turn-taking games

In PE lessons or on the playground, include games or activities which have a turn-taking element as often as you can, in order to help the child understand the concept.

- Teach the child, through games, that it is fun to play together in groups and that waiting their turn (in anticipation) can also be enjoyable.
- Simply play some music and instruct each child, pair or a small group to move around to the music in turn.
- Teach the children to play games such as 'Duck, Duck, Goose'. This can be played with five or more children.
  - Sit in a circle.
  - Explain that the aim of the game is to end up as a 'Duck'.
  - Select 'Goose 1' who walks around the circle lightly touching each of the others' shoulders, saying '*duck*' each time.
  - Goose 1 then chooses to say '*goose*' on touching another child. Goose 2 then gets up and chases Goose 1 around the circle, aiming to sit in their place.
  - The first child to reach Goose 2's place sits down. Whoever is left standing becomes the new Goose 1.
  - The game continues in this fashion.

Using role-play to explore emotions

Provide a variety of role-play experiences for the child to establish their preferred mediums for expressing themselves.

- Imitation of everyday activities in an area of the classroom such as the 'home corner' can be extended by adult questioning or suggestions such as, '*How will Joe feel if you offer to help him wash up?*'
- Use puppets as a vehicle for the child to speak through and behave in a particular way, or for you to communicate with the child. '*Rabbit is feeling sad today* [paws over eyes, head down] *so how can we help him feel happy?*'
- Use a puppet that doesn't speak and question the child about how they think Rabbit is feeling.
- Use the role-play to explore the idea of things Rabbit likes/dislikes and things that make Rabbit feel happy or cross. Once the child can do this for Rabbit and other puppets, see if they can do it for themselves.

Asking to join a group

Use small world characters/role-play/ puppets/ stories and so on to explore ways of joining a group and of dealing with different possible responses.

Agree a class script so that all children know:

- how to ask to join a group;
- how to respond '*yes*' or '*no*' politely;
- how to deal with the response.

Establish a class/school expectation that people can join in a game if they ask nicely and agree to follow the rules. Agree a limited number of exceptions to that expectation (such as the need for equal teams in a football game).

Jigsaw puzzles

Provide a wide range of puzzles with a varying number of pieces and levels of complexity to suit the child and the task. Puzzles can be commercially or school-produced; you could use pictures and photos to make your own. At first, you help the child to complete a jigsaw, then introduce one other child, then another (depending on the complexity of the jigsaw).

- The child is encouraged to feel part of a group or team collaborating on a 'project' together.
- The project could have a problem-solving basis if the puzzle is a mystery object that reveals itself only when a certain number of pieces are placed.
- Model using socially appropriate language for working in a group. For example: '*Can you help me to ... ?*'; '*Thank you for ...*'; '*I think it's your turn to ...*'; '*Can I help you by ...?*'

Aspect 5: Social interactions with peers

Letter	Sharing/taking turns	Working as part of a group	Friendship skills	Dealing with disputes
E	With support, waits for their turn during a simple game against one other person without making a fuss	Knows that they have to wait longer for a turn when working in a group rather than a pair	Has fun with one or two friends	Will stay in one place for up to 5 minutes as directed by the teacher
E	Waits for their turn during a simple game against one other person without making a fuss	With support, waits for a turn during a small-group activity without a fuss	Has fun with friends in the classroom and playground	Knows that the teacher expects them to stay in one place as directed
F	Understands that a consequence of not waiting for their turn as expected may result in the loss of their turn	Waits for a turn during a small-group activity without a fuss	Describes *friendly* actions	Asks the teacher for help if they are unsure or upset in the classroom
F	Accepts a consequence (e.g. losing a turn or a minute of playtime)	Waits for the 'talking object' in Circle Time before speaking	Recognises the likes and dislikes of friends	Knows who to ask for help if they are unsure or upset in the playground
G	Is aware that the attention of the teacher or a friend has to be shared	Accepts changes of membership within a work group	With support, identifies characters in books who are/are not *friendly*, *lonely*, and do/do not *belong*	Is able to say '*sorry*', when prompted, if they upset another child
G	Is aware that school equipment has to be shared	Is aware that the members of the group share all equipment and resources on their table	Gets on well with most children in the class	Is able to say '*sorry*' unprompted, and mean it, if they upset another child
H	Takes turns with equipment during activities	With support, identifies the theme of 'co-operation' in stories (e.g. traditional tales such as 'Stone Soup')	Accepts friends' suggestions for games or modifications to the rules	Recognises when another child is unsure or upset
H	Listens, in turn, to others making suggestions for games or classroom activities	With support, identifies ways in which the group can co-operate to achieve a task	Says one thing that they think makes someone 'a *good friend*'	Feels able to say '*no*' to another child

Suggested activities or strategies

Rules for listening

Agree, and display in your classroom, some rules for listening. Accompany the rules with labelled photographs of children listening.

Initially, establish that 'good listening' means that:

- my eyes are looking at you;
- my ears are listening to you;
- my lips are closed;
- my hands and feet are still.

Once children have learned the basic rules of good listening, add expectations of listening in a group:

- I look at the speaker;
- I think about what they are saying;
- I wait until they have finished speaking before I speak;
- What I say should link to what the other speaker said.

A 'friendship book'

Create a 'friendship book' and ask children to write in the book when other people have done something that is kind or friendly. For example: *'He let me play with him'*; *'She helped me to find my coat'*; *'He said something nice to me'*; *'She was kind to me when I was feeling sad'*.

Read aloud from the book and ask children who wrote, as well as those who were written about, how they felt at the time. This will establish a clear understanding of what 'friend' and 'friendship' mean and create opportunities for recognising children who are kind and friendly. Make the book available at all times in the class.

Saying 'no'

The child may gain the confidence to say *'no'* when invited to take part in inappropriate activity, if it is explained to them that this is a skill that can be learned. If they feel confident in saying *'no'* in a variety of ways, they will be more inclined to make the right choices when interacting with peers.

- Begin by asking the child to think of choices they make regularly such as: following or breaking rules; being honest or telling a lie; being kind or unkind to other children.
- Ask the child to try to remember when they were asked to do something they didn't want to do such as: disobey an adult looking after them; tease another child; go where they were not allowed.
- Tell the child that, to stay safe and keep out of trouble, they must think about what could happen if they did as requested. Explore the consequences of bad choices and how they can be avoided by saying *'no'* in different ways.
- Teach the child ways of saying *'no'* according to the circumstances and encourage them to think of other ways themself.
  - *'If I did ... my mum would be really unhappy.'*
  - *'I try to be nice to people so I don't want to do ...'*
  - *'I'm not allowed to go to ... but I would like to play football in the park with you.'*

You can find a useful article by Leah Davies about teaching children 'refusal skills' at www.kellybear.com/teacherarticles/teachertip21.html.

Share stories

One of the most powerful ways of exploring emotions is through the stories you share with your class. Whatever age the children are, there will be stories – in books, films, DVDs – in which characters experience emotions.

- Pause the story-telling and ask children to predict how a character is feeling.
- Explore how emotions and responses are described in books.
- Freeze a DVD and look at a character's body language and facial expression. Encourage children to talk about how you can tell that someone is feeling upset.
- Display pictures from the story or stills from the DVD, together with words and sentences that describe how the character is feeling.

Aspect 5: Social interactions with peers

Letter	Sharing/taking turns	Working as part of a group	Friendship skills	Dealing with disputes
I	With support, accepts that suggestions, thoughts or ideas can be shared with others	Accepts group rules as directed by the teacher	Suggests ideas for games to friends	Offers appropriate comment when another child is unsure or upset
I	With support, accepts that listening to others enables sharing	Suggests own ideas for group rules which apply to a particular activity	With support, makes suggestions about things that make someone a good friend	Asks an adult's help for another child
J	With support, listens to another child 'having their say' without interrupting	Accepts group rules, agreed by the group members, which apply to a particular activity	Says positive things about most other children in the class	Names feelings *angry*, *surprised*, *disappointed*, *scared* and demonstrates understanding of what they mean
J	Accepts that worries can be shared with others	Is aware that, within the group, people may be given different jobs to do	Accepts being directed to work with someone with whom they do not usually work or play	Responds appropriately to being reprimanded by the teacher
K	Is willing to share worries with an adult	Is willing to take responsibility for part of a shared task as directed	Plays co-operatively even when a game is not of their choosing	Uses '*I*' statements to express needs and feelings if in dispute with other children
K	Accepts that decision-making can be shared if everyone involved has their say	Accepts responsibility if they make a mistake	Accepts public praise and positive comments about themselves	Seeks the help of an adult when they feel unable to manage a dispute with another child
L	Accepts that others do not always share their views	With support, recognises that mistakes help them learn	Is willing to include in games other children outside their immediate friendship circle	Accepts the intervention and direction of an adult even when unhappy with it
L	Offers support to others whose views they share in a decision-making process	Suggests ways of achieving a group task	On occasions, will ask to join in games with children outside their immediate friendship circle	Shows resilience when other children are upset with them, by trying to identify what has gone wrong

Suggested activities or strategies

Learning to listen without interrupting

Pair up the child with a classmate, either on their own or within a group/class setting of pairs.

- Tell each child that they must speak to their partner for 2 minutes and describe something they like to do and why.
- The listener then has to tell you what was described to them.
- Congratulate the child for being a good listener.
- Ask the children to swap roles, so that the other listens.

Group roles

Prepare the child to accept and understand that the roles of group members vary from day to day and task to task.

- At the beginning of the school year, direct the whole class to think of group work rules. Once these are decided, display them clearly.
- Spend time outlining the different roles within groups that the children will be asked to undertake.
- Explore what the children think is involved in the roles and make cards that can be used to prompt the child adopting a particular role.
- It is important that the child experiences each role, so rotate jobs.
- Teach children that all group members are expected to behave respectfully, and teach them how to:
  - support someone else's opinion, adding new information;
  - disagree with what someone said, explaining reasons for the disagreement.

Developing resilience

We all find it difficult to 'recover' when something goes wrong, but it is important that we learn to accept responsibility for our actions. Teach children the following rules about how to participate in conversations about what has gone wrong:

- Listen respectfully to what the other person says.
- Ask them to listen to you.
- Look at them and, if you can, make eye contact while you are talking.
- Speak clearly. It is hard to listen if someone is mumbling or shouting.
- Use 'I' statements to take the blame away from the other person: '*I felt angry when …*', '*I didn't think it was fair when …*'.

Ask the child to suggest what should happen next. Congratulate all children who follow these rules in sorting out disputes.

Exploring friendships

Use a 'snowball' technique (children work in pairs, then pairs join to make fours, then fours join to make eights, and so on) to explore children's attitudes to friendship through statements such as:

- '*I won't be your friend unless you always play with me and only me.*'
- '*I won't be your friend if you play with him/her.*'
- '*If you play with other people, you can't be my friend.*'

Having explored the children's responses to those statements, discuss what the implications could be for playtime.

Games that encourage co-operation

- Lining up:
  - tell the children they must not talk to each other but can mime or sign;
  - instruct them to line up according to a theme such as birth month or alphabetical order of names.
- Leading the blind: the child leads a blindfold classmate around, explaining where they are going and what to expect.
- Alphabet art: split the class into groups of six to eight. Tell them you will call out a letter and each group is to form a body sculpture of the letter. Give each group 20 seconds to make their crab, seaweed, dolphin, wave.

Aspect 5: Social interactions with peers

Letter	Sharing/taking turns	Working as part of a group	Friendship skills	Dealing with disputes
M	Identifies those with whom they share common interests, who may not be friends	Works collaboratively with others and is an effective communicator in group discussions	Explores friendships with a wider range of peers	With support, distinguishes between passive, aggressive and assertive approaches
M	Shares activities and interests with those who may not be friends	Is willing to join in with new groups in and out of school	Uses vocabulary such as *thoughtful*, *patient*, *trustworthy*, *understanding* to describe a friend	Understands that restorative approaches may help in the aftermath of a dispute
N	Is able to think confidently about aspects they share and do not share with others	Is aware of strengths and skills they may contribute to a new group	Volunteers to train to be a 'playground buddy' or similar role	Models assertive approaches (such as eye contact, posture, tone of voice, 'I' statements) in role-play or drama lessons
N	Begins to make decisions, based on shared friendships and interests, about how they could manage their free time in and out of school	Engages in a variety of group activities in and out of school	Accepts that different friends may have different qualities	Is appropriately assertive in their dealings with others

Suggested activities or strategies

Passive, aggressive, assertive

Use role-play scenarios to model and discuss different ways of expressing and responding to strongly felt emotions and desires. Emphasise the fact that strong feelings are appropriate and shared by everyone, but that we are responsible for the choices we make about how to communicate these feelings.

Following role-play, discuss responses to different kinds of behaviour:

- **Cool, assertive** (a person who is polite, friendly, calm, in control, confident).
- **Weak** (a person who mumbles, is led by others, is indecisive).
- **Aggressive** (a person who shouts, threatens, is rude, seems angry and out of control).

Encourage the group to share their insights about the effectiveness of each approach. Explore strategies for:

- sharing a strong emotion;
- dealing with someone who is sharing a strong emotion.

Use quizzes to explore cool, weak and aggressive responses to scenarios, for example:

- Someone calls you names. What do you do? a) push them; b) get upset; c) ignore them.
- Someone calls you names. What are a) cool; b) weak; or c) aggressive ways to react?

Joining new groups

- Encourage the child to take part in extra-curricular activities that are organised by the school, and suggest to parents/carers that joining a club, team or any structured adult-led activity outside school benefits the child and can provide scope for expanding friendship groups and raising self-esteem.
- Encourage persistence and 'stickability'. If you are told that the child becomes bored or wants to drop activities early on, stress the importance of insisting that the child sees at least one activity through.
- Celebrate the child's achievements in their extra-curricular activities: the winning goal for the town team; the orange belt in karate. The child may swell with pride if their name is mentioned in assembly or, if they are reluctant to accept this level of acknowledgement, a whispered word of praise to them alone may be as rewarding.

Different people, different strengths

Talk with the children about *'what I want from a good friend'*. Help them to make lists of their responses. Ask whether they think that all of the qualities are likely to be found in one person.

- Ask them to write a list of their friends, and to note which of the qualities each person has.
- If there are children in the group who don't have a social circle in school, do the activity using a character in a film or book.
- Establish the fact that we need to develop different relationships with different people: the person who is sensitive about your feelings and who will keep your secrets may not be the same person who you play football with in the playground.
- Encourage children to value different friends for the different qualities they bring to the friendship.

Aspect 6: Managing transitions

Letter	Readiness for change	Accepting the need for change	Moving on	Managing new situations and new people
A	Seems to be happy/have fun in school at least once a week	With support, stays in the playground/classroom	With support, separates from parent/carer calmly	Looks in teacher's direction when spoken to
A	Names feelings *happy*, *sad* and demonstrates awareness of what they mean	Stays in the playground/classroom	Separates from parent/carer calmly	Knows teacher's name
B	Identifies something or someone, in school, that makes them feel happy	With support, sits on carpet tile or seat	Walks into school holding an adult's hand	Understands that they are included when the teacher addresses the whole class
B	Leaves 'comfort' toy from home in a special place for most of the school day	Sits on carpet tile/seat as directed	Walks into school holding another child's hand	Responds when their name is called
C	Names feelings *OK* and *angry* and demonstrates awareness of what they mean	Is aware that activity differs in some areas of the classroom (e.g. reading in the book corner)	With support, moves to different classroom areas as directed	Interacts with peers at a basic level (e.g. '*It's your turn*')
C	Chooses a resource or activity, such as a book from the book corner to read	Names and indicates the different areas of the classroom	Moves to different classroom areas as directed	Remembers names of classmates
D	Says what they enjoy doing	Follows routines for entering and leaving the classroom	Starts task as requested by an adult sitting alongside	With support, uses a timer to sustain concentration for 4 minutes on a specific task
D	Identifies something they would like to do that they have not yet tried	Follows routines for movement around the classroom	Starts task when whole class is directed by the teacher	Uses a timer without support to sustain concentration for 4 minutes on a specific task

Suggested activities or strategies

Establish routines

Be aware that parents/carers can be anxious about leaving their child at school for the first time and that the child may pick up on this feeling.

- Talk to the parents about planning the transition from home to school.
- On the first day of school, consider allowing the parent/carer to come into class with the child while you show them where coats are left and where the toilet is and how the child is expected to begin the day: on the carpet; playing in the home corner; or whatever routines are being established. Support a firm, cheerful separation: '*Mummy will give you a kiss now as we are going to have a story*'.
- If a routine for separation is agreed between you, aim to shorten it over time.
- Encourage the parent/carer to be clear about who is to collect the child after school so any reassurances you make during the day are realised: '*...Granddad will be so pleased that you finished your painting when he sees you after school*'.

Staying on task

If a child is wasting a lot of time wandering around the classroom instead of starting an activity, consider the following:

- First find out what the problem is. It may be that the child does not feel confident that they can do the work. If your main target is for them to start work when requested, reduce the demands of the work to a task in which they can easily succeed.
- Give the child their own 'tool kit' at the place where they are working, in order to reduce the need to wander to find a sharp pencil, or a pair of scissors.
- Make sure that the child knows when they can finish.
- Establish a reward which will follow successful – and high-quality – completion of this task.
- Use a timer. Explain that the timer will show the amount of time the child is losing from the reward activity by wasting time now.

Becoming part of a class

Children who don't access pre-school can find it difficult to develop an identity as part of a group; previously they have always been named individually.

Initially, name the child when you want them to join the class in doing something: '*Everyone stand still. Nathan you need to stand still too.*'

Gradually, use non-verbal signals, such as making eye contact, instead of saying the name, to anticipate compliance.

Selecting activities

Some children access only a limited range of the activities on offer. To widen their horizons try the following:

- Take photographs/use symbols for the different activities available on a day.
- Offer a limited range – of which only two should be familiar.
- Ask the child to choose three pictures of things they are going to do.
- Provide a 3/5-minute timer, and establish the expectation that the child will stay at each activity at least until the timer has run out.
- Once they have done the activity, the child can 'post' their picture in a box.
- Initially, the child may need a reminder that there is only 1 minute left of a familiar activity before they transfer to a new one.

Using timers

Use timers to encourage high-quality work, by the simple expedient of putting the timer over on its side when the work is not being done to your satisfaction and turning it back again when the child starts to work as you have asked.

- Initially, keep expectations of focused time working to a minimum, with a clear and desirable reward.
- Make expectations and sanctions clear.
- Congratulate the child when they have achieved their target even if there have been lots of 'time outs'.

Aspect 6: Managing transitions

Aspect 6: Managing transitions

Letter	Readiness for change	Accepting the need for change	Moving on	Managing new situations and new people
E	Brings in objects from home in which they have an interest	Describes, to the teacher, their interest in objects brought from home	Calmly leaves a task for completion at a later time, as directed	With support, takes turns in games with at least one other child
E	Knows that taking part in a game is fun even if they don't win	Tells someone that they liked playing a turn-taking game even if they lost	Returns to an unfinished task after a period of time	Takes turns in games without support
F	Describes changes to themselves through sequencing personal photos	Describes how, by changing as they grow, they have become able to do more things	Uses a visual timetable, or Now and Next board, to anticipate changes	Personalises a visual timetable with symbols of their choosing
F	Identifies characters in books who grow and change	Describes how characters in books become able to do more things	Sets themselves a target of trying something different (e.g. eating a new food at lunchtime)	Enjoys playtimes and has fun with friends
G	Uses words which describe transitions (e.g. *growing, changing, new, different, exciting, interesting*)	Anticipates future changes for themselves (e.g. says '*When I am 7 I will be able to...*')	With support, sets themselves a goal or target to achieve today	Co-operates with another child to achieve a task in class with no adult support
G	Identifies with some characters in books whose transitions are *different, exciting* and *interesting*	Talks of changes about which they are excited or which may be of interest	Evaluates progress towards the goal or target	Asks to be included in group play in the playground, using the 'social script' provided (see page 91)
H	Suggests what may be different about their next year's class (e.g. new teacher, new classroom)	Talks of changes that may help them to make progress in their next year's class	Accepts an offer of help from an adult to assist them towards their goal or target	Uses a timer independently to mark the beginning and end of a task in class
H	Says things they think they can do well	Says what things they will do better with the change of year group	Accepts praise and works towards rewards	Gets on well with most children in the class

Suggested activities or strategies

Show and tell

The child can be encouraged to share objects brought in from home with the class, to demonstrate that what they value is important to you and the other children.

- Another adult could support the child by rehearsing, with them, a short description of the object and its use and importance.
- The child could be asked to talk about an event or outing instead of an object.
- If the child is anxious about talking to the whole class, they could talk to a small group.
- You could suggest, 'I think that is a very interesting book/picture. Shall we share it with "Mrs Headteacher" in her office?'

Social scripts

The child may need a structured approach to feel confident in attempting social interactions in the playground. A script can provide a way of helping the child understand social expectations.

- Ask the child for their ideas as to what to do first and keep the script simple: *'You will walk towards the group who are skipping ... you will watch them for a little while ... you will call the name of someone you know, once they have stopped skipping ...'.*
- Use role-play and/or puppets to rehearse the script.
- Relax the child with humour.
- Ask the parent or carer to rehearse the script at home.

Descriptive praise

Be conscious of the type of praise you are using with the child. Evaluative praise consists of *'That's great/brilliant ... good work ... you have done well!'* and is generic. Descriptive praise, which helps the child know how to repeat the desired behaviour, describes what the child is doing. For example, *'I like the way you're lining up. You're looking forwards and leaving a space between you and the person in front'*.

Descriptive praise, used consistently, encourages the child to form their own judgements and helps them develop into an independent learner. However, be aware that some children find it hard to accept praise, because earning praise doesn't fit with their self-image. These children are likely to sabotage the praise, for example, by destroying the work you have just been so positive about. For these children, agree a small signal (such as a thumbs up, or a smiley face drawn on a piece of work) to use instead of verbal praise until the child is ready to accept praise spoken aloud.

Pupil passports

A pupil passport is a particularly powerful tool for transition because it records the child's voice. Pupil passports can extend from a single page of A4 to a 12-page booklet. Look for templates online, or create your own.

Minimally, the pupil passport should include:

- The child's name and photograph.
- The child's views of:
  - what I enjoy and what I'm good at;
  - what I need help with;
  - what helps me with my learning;
  - what makes it more difficult for me to learn;
  - how I communicate what I'm feeling.

The pupil passport should be shared with the child's new teaching team and with any supply teachers or cover supervisors. It should be updated when the information is out of date.

Aspect 6: Managing transitions

Letter	Readiness for change	Accepting the need for change	Moving on	Managing new situations and new people
I	Says things they think they are not good at	Responds positively when told, by the teacher, that they are *'going to learn something new today'*	With support, splits simple tasks into achievable chunks	Co-operates with other children in a small group to achieve a task in class
I	Accepts making a mistake in their work, calmly	Corrects mistakes in their work without a fuss	Independently splits simple tasks into achievable chunks	Co-operates in small groups when the composition of the group changes
J	Listens to the teacher explaining something a second time if the first explanation has not been understood	Accepts verbal correction of work or behaviour from the teacher	Sets themselves a goal or target to achieve today	Resists some distractions for 5 minutes
J	Accepts that something not understood can become clear when left for another time	Accepts that a temporary change of task can help them learn better	Changes tasks, if advised	Speaks positively about most of the others in the class
K	Names feelings *worried*, *proud*, *determined*, *hopeful* and demonstrates understanding of meanings	Understands that worrying about not being able to do something does not stop them trying	Adapts to new classroom rules and routines	Takes responsibility for own actions
K	Is willing to 'have a go' at something they are unsure of achieving	Talks to adults about their worries and hopes for the change of year group	Shows determination to try something new	Is helpful and considerate towards adults and children in the class

92   *The Target Ladders*

© *Target Ladders: BESD*   LDA   Permission to Photocopy

Suggested activities or strategies

The language of goal-setting

Familiarise the child with the concepts and vocabulary associated with setting goals and targets.

- '*Plan*', with the class, a collective goal to achieve over a short period of time, such as putting together a class newsletter.
- Discuss the '*steps needed*' to achieve this goal.
- Display the results of this discussion as a '*target*' staircase, then tell the children to write '*Achieved*' at the top once steps are accomplished.
- Emphasise that a child may have to '*wait*' to achieve a step or '*overcome*' a difficulty (such as the printer running out of ink, or corrections being required in a piece of work).
- Congratulate the children on every step achieved '*towards the goal*'.
- Ask individual children to set themselves a goal and identify the steps needed.
- Celebrate the achievement of the goal and involve parents/carers and colleagues.

Community challenge

Encourage the child to 'have a go' at something new or challenging by establishing a 'Challenge board' in the classroom. Refresh the challenges frequently and include a range of activities. Suggest challenges to the child if they are reluctant to choose for themselves. Include:

- Physical challenges, such as skipping a certain number of times in the playground.
- Social challenges, such as asking someone they don't know well to play with them.
- Community challenges, such as creating healthy eating posters or slogans to display in the dining hall.
- Academic challenges, such as finding as many words as possible using the letters of a long word or multiplying large numbers without using a calculator.

Community responsibility

Cultivate an expectation of the child that they will undertake a role of responsibility which benefits the whole class. Explain that you are depending on the child to carry out this role. This encourages the child to develop skills of leadership and responsibility towards the community.

- The child is to be aware that others in the class also have roles of responsibility.
- The role should be within the child's capability, but with an element of challenge.

The child's role could be to become the class librarian, in charge of book loans and records and making sure the library area is tidy. Or the child could be in charge of making sure the correct equipment is ready on tables for certain lessons. The child may have their own ideas as to what could be a suitable role for themselves.

Managing anxiety

- Encourage children to use the trusting relationships they have developed with the adults this year to share worries and concerns about a major transition to a new class or a new school.
- Allow the children to work in small groups with an adult acting as a 'listening ear'.
- The adult should explain to the children that everyone is nervous of change and we have to learn to manage our anxieties.
- Through discussion, help to identify the main anxieties and to sort them into three groups:
  ○ for me [that is, the child] to manage;
  ○ for someone else to manage;
  ○ can't do anything about it.
- Agree how to share the anxieties that are for other people to manage. Talk about the fact that we have to accept that there are some things we can't change, so there's no point in worrying.
- Help the children to focus on what they need to manage. Use strategies for goal-setting (described above) to identify what the issue is and what the steps are to manage it.

Aspect 6: Managing transitions

Letter	Readiness for change	Accepting the need for change	Moving on	Managing new situations and new people
L	Shows resilience if something goes wrong	Is willing to try again when something goes wrong	Recognises that achievement is sometimes a series of small steps	With support, manages to bring books and equipment/kit to school
L	With support, works out a solution to a problem	With support, identifies the steps needed to reach a solution	Attempts a step towards a solution	With support, organises books and equipment/kit in school
M	Works out a solution to a problem	Identifies the steps needed to reach a solution	Independently takes steps towards a solution	Identifies, collects and manages resources relevant to a task
M	Anticipates changes in routine without worrying (e.g. having a different teacher for a short time)	Accepts the need for unexpected changes in routine	Adapts to an unexpected change in routine	Manages to persevere with tasks that are unwelcome or unexpected
N	Has the confidence to put themselves forward for a role of responsibility	Is aware that participating in aspects of school beyond regular routines and activities reaps long-term rewards	Involves themselves in a variety of activities in and out of school	Manages and organises personal books and equipment independently
N	Carries out duties of assigned roles with competence and confidence	Anticipates the positive aspects of moving to secondary school	Takes leading roles in some activities in and out of school	Is welcoming and accepting of new staff and class members

Suggested activities or strategies

A solution-focused approach

The aim is to encourage the child to view problems as solvable and to equip them to identify steps towards solutions. The approach revisits some of the 'Language of goal-setting' activities on page 93. A session for a solution-focused approach might include:

Focus on the positive:

- Talk about the good things: what has gone well; what the child is proud of having achieved; what makes them feel good.

Talk about exceptions to feeling negative about a change in routine:

- Can the child think of any occasion when a change in routine was welcome? Perhaps birthdays, Christmas, holidays, a time when they were promised a surprise or when a different teacher taught a fun lesson?
- Talk about what was different about the occasion when a change in routine felt OK.
- Encourage the child to produce the answers and think about what they did, what was involved, how much they wanted to participate, and so on.

Identify a goal and scale it:

- From this conversation, can the child identify their own immediate goal?
- If not, develop the conversation and listen to what the child is saying about how they feel about a change in routine.
- Agree what a good goal would be. Draw a line from 1 to 10, where 10 is achieving the goal and doing it easily and well, and 0 is nowhere near it, can't do it, it's too hard.
- Ask the child to tell you where on the line they think they are now.
- Can they also identify where they think they would need to get to in order to feel OK about this aspect of their learning?
- If the child scales themselves now more than one or two points below where they think they would like to be, revisit the goal and simplify it. The idea is to achieve the goal.

Agree what it would look like and feel like to achieve the goal:

- Use the magic wand test. Imagine that someone waved a magic wand this minute and the goal was achieved.
  - How would you know what had changed?
  - Who else would know?
  - How would they know?
  - How would you know they knew?
- Use discussions arising from the questions to encourage the child to describe the situation they would like to see. This, then, is the long-term goal, but now the child has defined it and understands what it would look and feel like.

Finish the session:

In order to finish the session on a positive note:

- Congratulate the child on something they have done or said and explain why you are pleased.
- Agree specific tasks for the child to do between this session and the next one. The tasks should relate closely to the child's goal and their response to the magic wand question.

There are a variety of books offering more information about using a solution-focused approach, including: John Rhodes and Yasmin Ajmal, *Solution Focused Thinking in Schools: Behaviour, Reading and Organisation* (1995) London, BT Press.

Links to other *Target Ladders* titles

Other books in the *Differentiating for Inclusion* series may well include targets that will be appropriate for some children with BESD. For example:

Target Ladders: Autistic Spectrum
Louise Nelson

Includes additional targets for:
- Personal organisation
- Getting attention
- Social interaction
- Managing feelings

Target Ladders: Dyslexia
Kate Ruttle

Includes additional targets for:
- Planning, organising and remembering
- Self-confidence and motivation

Target Ladders: Speech, Language and Communication Needs
Susan Lyon et al.

Includes additional targets for:
- Attention control
- Comprehension
- Social communication
- Pragmatic understanding

Other useful resources from LDA

Forest of Feelings: Understanding and exploring emotions – 2nd edition
Carol Holliday and Jo Browning Wroe

Goal Maker: Learning to set and achieve realistic goals
Amanda Kirby and Lynne Peters

How to Support Children Moving School
Mike Fleetham

Quality Circle Time in the Primary Classroom
Jenny Mosley

Socially Speaking (book and game)
Alison Schroeder

Special Games: Adaptable activities for personal and social development
Betty Rudd

Time to Talk
Alison Schroeder

Turn Your School Round
Jenny Mosley